I0140273

HUMANUS-REBELDE
ACAPULCO-NEW YORK

LATIN AMERICAN POLITICAL CINEMA

Jorge Majfud

HUMANUS

SAN DIEGO-ACAPULCO

Latin American Political Cinema
University of Georgia 2005
© by Jorge Majfud 2025
© Humanus 2025
Humanus | humanus.info
Email: editor@humanus.info
ISBN: 978-1-956760-33-0
All rights reserved. No part of this book may be reproduced or used in any form or by any means—graphic, electronic, or mechanical, including photocopying, recording, or information storage and retrieval systems—without written permission from the copyright owner.

INDEX

MEMORIES OF FORGETTING

Utopia, Resistance, and Despair
(1968-2003)

"The mere existence of a Latin American film is already an act
of resistance"
Ignacio Ramonet, Le Monde Diplomatique, 2003

I. Introduction

The Brothel and Social Commitment

Irwin R. Blacker, a professor of famous screenwriters like
Bob Gale1, in his guide to creating successful films, wrote:
"The premise is the basis of the conflict. The premise must
be clear to the writer before he begins to write." (Blacker,
6) "The viewer needs to know why a character acts as he
does —his motivation. There must be a logical inevitability
to his actions. What he does may be surprising, but when
considered, it must make sense, it must be rational" (35)
The viewer has been watching to see how the conflict will
be resolved. He may not like an unhappy resolution, but he
will like it considerably more than no resolution. (15).

---

[1] Bob Gale, screenwriter of *Back to the Future.*

The concern of *how* a film is made is typical of writers, producers, and directors in Hollywood. A good *how* —and, with it, the star— guarantees success —sales, profitability, earnings—. However, the concern of the New Latin American Cinema has been, if not entirely, at least as an identifying characteristic, a greater concern about the why and the what for. If the how interrogates the techniques of filmmaking and maintains a complacent dialogue with its audience, the why will interrogate power relations, sustaining a critical and accusatory dialogue with the society of which it is a part. The how needs to create a conflict and resolve it within the projection room, in the same way that sex begins and ends in a brothel. From there, the client will leave satisfied and ready for production, without taking away any lasting memories of the woman who pretended to love him. In contrast, the why does not seek to invent a conflict or resolve it within the projection room, as it assumes that this conflict predates its writing and currently exists in society—the relations of domination, ethical reflection, historicism, class struggle, transparent ideologies, etc. Therefore, the conflict must be resolved outside the dark room. In some cases, solutions are proposed; in others, the impossibility of such solutions is acknowledged—through art—and they merely limit themselves to exposing a specific social and individual problem.

While every film has a *why*, as it is produced within a specific ideological context —Mas'ud Zavarzaeh—, not all exercise the uncomfortable virtue of self-reflection. Films

8

that originate from a brilliant how generally reproduce their ideological context in a transparent manner. Without an effort of ocular adjustment —a "critical" adjustment, for which the viewer is usually not predisposed— the viewer will never be able to perceive it. Like other traditions of European cinema, the New Latin American Cinema was born and developed with the intention of multiple readings, many of which consisted of a critical look at its own ideological context, the power relations that structure the societies from which it emerges. Inevitably, its semiotics had to be open, interrogative. There can be no final resolution —ideological orgasm— because it is not confined to the rules of art itself. Its greatest virtue is interrogation, transcendence beyond the cinematic fact: the rescue of collective memory. But there is no collective memory without critique, as other narratives intervene in its construction, a counterpoint often perverse with specialized forgetting.

With this intention, for this intellectual exercise, it drew on many elements, various revisions. One of them, as it could not be otherwise, has been related to a deeply felt Latin American obsession: memory.

In these notes, I will trace the dramatic process of transformation that collective memory has undergone in Latin America through some of its most celebrated and resisted films. The existence of three important stages seems evident:

>   I.   *Time of social utopia.*
>   II. *Time of resistance and denunciation.*
>   III. *Time of defeat and nihilism.*

Each stage, as it could not be otherwise, is related to the ideologies vying for power.

The process will also show the evolution of a defeat that goes from action to emotional and ideological aspects. However, it is not confined solely to a number of filmmakers with particular ideologies, but extends to the social context from which it arises.

In summary, this dramatic social and artistic process will be nothing other than the unequal dialogue of the region —Latin America— with the ideological, economic, and military center of the world. Latin American identity itself is defined in relation to its older siblings, in a conflictive manner, with resentment and admiration, with demonstrations of rebellion and submission, of youthful maturity and senile amnesia.

II. From Utopia to Resistance

Shortly before the beginning of the decade of the "end of history," Alfredo Guevara said: "In 1967, we did not perceive any possible contradiction between art and militancy, the latter word with contexts and subtexts that wrongly equated it to a dulling anti-artistic routine" (*Cuadernos de Cine Número* 33, 7). Around the same time, during the IX

International Festival of New Latin American Cinema in Havana, Paul Ledux, from Mexico, said: "And if Brecht wrote years ago 'What times these are in which it is criminal to speak of the beauty of trees,' they proposed changing the phrase of that German exiled in Hollywood and making it so that only the beauty of trees was spoken of." Later, paraphrasing the shortest story in history, by Monterroso, he warns of a present that is nothing more than the miserable continuation of the past: "And when he awoke, misery was still visible through the window." (22, 23)

Significant was also what Miguel Littin, from Chile, expressed. On that occasion, he recalled the first and now mythical Viña del Mar Festival (1967), where he himself had proclaimed: "Cinema in Latin America should not follow the European or North American path. This is not a festival of stars but of achievements." (35)

The "star" is a product of the bourgeoisie, of capitalist consumerism, of fetishistic idolatry and forgetfulness, while "achievements," that experimental and auteur cinema, should be critical and revolutionary. However, Littin himself acknowledges, not without nostalgia: "In 1967 and in 1969, our dreams had no limits, our aspiration was total revolution, our spirit exploded in utopias; revolutionary victory seemed within reach." (36)

The threat of demobilization and forgetting is hinted at in the words of Jorge Sanjinés, from Bolivia: "It is not about infusing the burgeoning New Latin American Cinema with 'political religiosity.' Not at all, it is simply about not

11

losing, at any moment, the awareness of the grave historical moment we are living in our countries, not losing for a moment the awareness of the collective suffering endured by our peoples, because from this awareness we will draw strength, we will draw the will to oppose, with what we have at hand... [We must] reestablish the truly anti-imperialist character of the New Latin American Cinema. We should not be ashamed today of having upheld that postulate before." (55)

Here, it is no longer about reaching utopia, revolution, the ideal state of a future society, but about not succumbing to chaos, to the extensive defeat, *to forgetting*. This will be confirmed by Carlos Rebolledo, from Venezuela: "We are in a historical period of accumulated collective frustration" (74). As part of this forgetting, we understand the observation of a European, Peter B. Schumann, from what was then the Federal Republic of Germany: "How is it explained, then, that today there are almost no radical political films, not even documentaries, here in Latin America, where class contradictions are sharper, where hunger is even greater, repression more violent, exploitation more devastating? [...] Where are the films that ignite the fuse, as the third part of The Hour of the Furnaces did? [...] Moreover, in the democracies that have expanded in Latin America, there is rather a social democratic will for transformation among filmmakers instead of a revolutionary fire" (109). This is not surprising, since cinema, although it could be considered, like all art, a vanguard of social mobilizations, a critical and accusatory instrument, is also a reflection of the society in which it is immersed.

To conclude, Julio García Espinosa, from Cuba, recalled: "We defend a cinema that reconciles poetry and militancy. Because art, comrades, as we all know [...] is found equally among the apocalyptic and the integrated [...] among the reactionary and the revolutionary" (140).

In this brief period of time, we can appreciate the metamorphosis of memory and hope, from the militant confidence[2] of *The Hour of the Furnaces* (Argentina, Solanas and Getino, 1968) to the nihilistic skepticism of The Rose Seller (Colombia, Gaviria, 1998), thirty years later.

III. Memory for Utopia

Without memory, there is no consciousness. Therefore, memory will play a decisive role in this period that goes from Utopia to Resignation. In Memories of Underdevelopment by Tomás Gutiérrez Alea (Cuba, 1968), the dialectic of forgetting-memory takes on a political and economic significance that structures the entire reflective discourse of the film. After portraying Elena's psychology through

---

[2] Recently, Francisco Gómez Tarín (Gómez, 6) noted that when we speak of "revolutionary cinema" in Latin America, we are not referring to a purely artistic revolution —as might be the case with many of the European avant-garde movements of the early 20th century—, but rather to an interventionist cinema.

several scenes, Gutiérrez Alea turns to the direct reflection of the protagonist, Sergio, to finally explain, in a very direct manner, what had been sensed long before: Elena is Latin America, that inconstant, unstable woman who never matures in her character. As we see a summary of her physical attitudes, her gestures, Sergio laments her lack of consequence, consistency, and ability to accumulate experience. Cubans —Latin Americans— adapt to the moment. Elena is the image of underdevelopment —the opposite of Hanna, the German woman who flees the Nazi regime—: she is incapable of sustaining a feeling, and in this idea, there is a strong Nietzschean scent, a recurrence of will, character, instinct as a state of maturity. Nor has the character of the people reached maturity. In fact, it resists. In the trial for sexual abuse by Elena and her family, Sergio is acquitted by formal justice, but he emerges defeated from his experience with Elena's family (the people), which has shown all the strength of cultural rigidity. "I have seen too much to be innocent—reflects the protagonist—; they have too much darkness in their heads to be guilty."

Decades later, in a period of despair, in *Mujer transparente* (Cuba, 1990) —using contrast and flashback—, this amnesia responsible for failure becomes painfully clear: those who fled into exile during the time of utopia were labeled "human scum" or simply "worms," but now they returned as tourists and were considered "first class." The Cubans, like the protagonist, not only had no access to spaces reserved for the former worms, but where they were, they were treated with contempt —by their own compatriots, by the employees of those spaces. How was this possible if not through shameless amnesia?

Also in *Eva Perón* (Argentina, 1996), the protagonist, when confronting the workers, her people, resorts to the memory-forgetting game: the workers who strike against Perón have forgotten the benefits they received from him, which will make them weak or incapable of continuing the "revolution." The forgetting of oligarchic oppression also threatens this project.

IV. Amnesia for the End of History

The power of the ruling classes is not such if the dominated counterpart does not recognize the symbolic relationship —that precedes the material one— that binds them and, therefore, must constantly nourish the symbol. Power does not need arguments to sustain itself, but arguments can threaten it.

In turn, this symbolic relationship is based, above all, on a certain ethic and a certain belief. The belief can be religious or materialist; in both cases, it is a promise about a future achievement, whether the conquest of happiness or salvation from catastrophe. These beliefs, materialist or religious, are what make humans unique in nature: their present is not explained solely by their past but, above all, by their future. We are here today not only because yesterday we traveled in this direction, but, above all, because

15

tomorrow we think we will head somewhere else—our present has an *intention*.

But the future is also made of the past, just as the past is made of the future —of utopias. To dominate —an action proper to the present— means *to control* both the past and the future. And in both cases, memory is the objective, the raw material with which the dominant ideology will work. That is, memory must be constructed *for a specific purpose*; and to construct means to select, modify, place, clean, and discard.

V. In Search of Lost Memory

In Latin America, Art and Power are enemies. At least when we speak of Art and Power with capital letters. While crimes and genocides, disappearances and violations were perpetuated in the silence of Justice and even of societies, art —mainly literature and cinema— has taken on the challenge of remembering. It would suffice to recall some representative films in countries where impunity has marked the consciousness —or unconsciousness— of society. In this case, only some of the most viewed and discussed films produced in Argentina after the last military dictatorship (1976-1983): *La historia oficial*[3] (Puenzo, 1985), *Hay unos tipos abajo* (Alfaro y Filippelli, 1985), *La noche de los lápices*

---

[3] Oscar Award.

16

(Olivera, 1986), *La república perdida* (Pérez, 1986), *La deuda interna* (Pereira, 1988), *La amiga* (1989), *El lado oscuro* (Suárez, 1992), 1977, *Casa tomada* (Pilotti, 1997), *Por esos ojos* (Arijón y Martínez, 1997), *Garage Olimpo* (Bechis, 1999), *Botín de Guerra* (Blaustein, 1999), *Operación Walsh* (Gordillo, 2000), *Ni vivo ni muerto* (Ruiz, 2001), *Kamchatka*, etc.

The relationship between history and memory is complex and conflictive in any society and, probably, even more so in societies like those of the Río de la Plata. Especially when their most recent histories are marked by the worst human rights violations that Good Manners sought to hide behind the Savior Order.

But what should be remembered and what should be forgotten? Is it good to remember, or does it only serve to bind us to the past? Until now, questions of this nature have never been considered in official and public discourse without a heavy dose of ideological bias. At times, the political left has used memory for its own vindication; on the other hand, the right—self-defined, not without reason, as the eternal "center"—has manipulated forgetting as a way to expand its sphere of economic domination, under the threat of a "return to disorder" that, contradicting the Brazilian flag, prevents us from achieving "progress." And in this race toward progress—systematically confused with the materialist model of the first world—everything is valid. *Even forgetting.*

VI. Ideology of Forgetting

Mariana Pianca, in *The Politics of Dislocation (or Return to the Memory of the Future)*, reminds us that this ideology of forgetting—recognizable in postmodernity and, above all, with the meteoric rise of the legitimizers of power, of the current order, of the inevitable order, of the best of all possible worlds, of F. Fukuyama —is not new, but had already been warned about in 1966 by Ángel Rama4 under the name of "ideological appeasement" (Pianca 118).

In the case of the Río de la Plata, forgetting was organized by the political class and confirmed, in some way, by the resignation of a large part of the population. In Argentina it was called "Punto Final," and included the classic pardon that in immature societies, or those prone to hypocrisy, is always reserved for wholesale criminals. In Uruguay there wasn't even the opportunity to initiate trials against human rights violators, as a prior amnesty for subversives had to legitimize a subsequent amnesty for the military, which came with the Expiry Law of Punitive State, confirmed by the population in a referendum that divided the country into two. Here too, the words of Marina Pianca

---

4 Ángel Rama, magazine Marcha, Montevideo, May 20, 1966. Cited by Marina Pianca in The Politics of Dislocation (or Return to the Memory of the Future), in Collective Memory and Politics of Forgetting, Argentina and Uruguay, 1970-1990. Beatriz Viterbo Editora, Buenos Aires, 1997.

could be applied: "Those who stubbornly continued to ask, to investigate, seemed marked as subversive archaeologists, diggers of the dead, or simply provocateurs" (130).

Mariana Pianca says, recalling Eduardo Grünter, that we live in a world that is constructed and deconstructed based on "discursive facts." When "perception" and "discursive fact" come into contradiction, the discursive fact prevails, given that such discursive facts have been legitimized by hegemonic sectors that have managed to equate this discourse with the idea of development, progress, and success. Following Grünter, we fully agree: "the victory of a dominant culture and ideology is all the more powerful the more the process of its imposition has gone unnoticed" (123). This ideology of forgetting—recognizable in post-modernity and, above all, with the meteoric rise of the legitimizers of power, of the current order, of the inevitable order, of the best of all possible worlds of F. Fukuyama—is not new, but had already been warned about in 1966 by Ángel Rama.[5]

This dialectic is one of the foundations of the moral domination of our societies. But the structure of this domination is complex and composed of different levels, spheres of control that are not always concentric, do not always coincide, and generally overlap.

---

[5] Magazine *Marcha*, Montevideo, May 20, 1966: reflections on "ideological appeasement."

Two of these spheres, perhaps the most important for understanding our societies, relate to culture and ideology.

Let us look at them for a moment, more closely.

The first (culture) shapes and reflects the *sensibility* of peoples, being both object and subject at the same time; the second (ideology) frames and, at times, directs the *thought* that later translates into an organizational action with specific purposes. As far as we know, until now, every ideology has served the interests of a particular social group at the expense of another, which may be an ancient legacy of intertribal wars and the unavoidable class struggle. Rich over poor, men over women, whites over blacks, etc.

We can think that an ideology aims at the conquest of social power, control, and domination in the process of the evolution of the human spirit. (At another time, we have categorized "spirit" as the presence of the "other" in the individual and in society simultaneously. Without the other —alive or dead—, there is no human spirit. The "human self" is the composition of social and historical heritage, that is, cultural; the "animal self" —physical and psychological— is the only truly individual thing we humans possess).

In turn, power is the main narrator of history. Its narration describes its own actions and predicts them; it provokes them. The dominant ideology (the one that has managed to monopolize power) will be opposed by resistance ideologies, which, in general, will have to resort to the same instrument: morality, the legitimizing basis of any enterprise, just or unjust, democratic or despotic, peaceful or warlike. Of course, I mean that ethics is also an ideological construction. However, based on certain moral principles, we could say that the best possible ideology would be the one that oppresses the fewest people for the benefit of the greatest number [ideological coefficient tending to zero: $Ik=(Im/Imx)$; $Ik{\neq}0$, $Ik{\rightarrow}0$].

No matter how absolute it may be, power has never acted without ethical legitimization, whether it is religious, economic, financial, political, or military power. For absolute power, the rationality or ethical justice of a particular legitimizing discourse is of no importance: what matters is that the ethical discourse serves its interests. When it no longer serves it, it simply overrides it with a new discourse. Those who suffer or resist this power will only have the possibility of resorting to reason and the construction of justice, that is, to a new discourse based on the principles built by history —for our time: democracy, liberty, equality, fraternity. The dominant power will seek to integrate these principles into its discourse, but never into its actions, as they generally interfere with its interests. And these will always come first.

Culture is responsible for organizing the semiotic language, an omnipresent instrument that is monopolized by the dominant ideology. And we all know that there is nothing harder to see than what is everywhere.

The dominant ideology will be responsible for articulating a discourse that establishes what is good and what is evil (that is, in our time, progress and failure, order and violence, the patriotic and the unpatriotic, the war hero and the terrorist, etc.) Culture, on the other hand, will be responsible for translating that discourse into the local language —when the ideology comes from outside—, or it will have to expand it throughout the international community —when the discourse comes from an internal sector of it—. Generally, the main transmitting instrument of this discourse is the ruling class, first, and the political class, second. The dissident may be found within this second group, but it is difficult for them to infiltrate with any possibility into the first, without running the risk of being absorbed or expelled by its force. As Mas'ud Zavarzaeh develops, the dissident will end up becoming part of the tradition; by not representing a material critique of the prevailing order, they will become an integrated part of it6 (Zavarzaeh 152 and 225).

By appropriating the material of culture —of tradition—, the discourse of success —of the eternally new— must be identified with the characters who in the past were

---

6 "People may 'dissent', but dissent, it is implied, is really a form of adolescent political tantrums: one grows up and recovers from it or one regresses into life-long infantilism and is thus banished from the society of adults. (pg. 152) [Dissent] is ineffective because it is an idealistic distancing from the existing institutions of capitalism and not a materialist critique of its operations nor an intervention in its economic order and class organizations of culture." — Mas'ud Zavarzaeh, Seeing Films Politically, pg. 169. State University of New York Press, Albany, 1991. (pag. 255)

positive figures for the current culture, characters who, in turn, were drawn by the same prevailing ideology or by a past dominant ideology. Thus, when the ideology of the dominant male is weakened by a feminist —Marxist— counter-discourse, the hegemonic ideology will seek to appropriate that discourse for its own benefit. In this way, men, at times and in the right dose, are replaced by women, but the —economic, religious, and financial— domination of a certain class remains. The same will happen with the vindication of blacks. We will witness an obscene spectacle: the replacement of white men, from some of the more visible sectors of power, by black women. The cultural icons of postmodernity change while the structure of domination remains: the masses of Black populations continue to be submerged in the lowest strata of societies, masked by brilliant public exceptions.

To maintain an ancient structure of exploitation and domination while simultaneously identifying with modernity, progress, and success, postmodern capitalism must manipulate the cultural resources it has at its disposal at every moment. It must transcend the limits of its own cultural region, identifying itself with Liberty, Justice, Goodness, and Security. Its values must be presented as universal, no matter over which culture, over which religion it extends its Law. And, above all, it must convince us that there is no alternative to its model.

But there is. It is the Disobedient Society.

However, the alternative to a dominant ideology is not an opposing ideology that seeks to dethrone the first to impose itself, in turn, on the throne, at the center, as was the Marxist project. Even resistant ideologies, such as feminism, end up immobilizing the critical value of individuals in favor of a warlike apparatus. It is likely that this construction we call the Disobedient Society will eventually disappear at the hands of the Forces of Order or take on the characteristics of an ideology. But even in this case, it should become aware of and distance itself from the prejudices and harms that this transformation always entails: the dysfunction of free thought, radically critical, untamable —eternally young, because a mature society will have a young spirit or will return to the obedience of its childhood; paradoxically, to the obedience of a new ideology.

Bertolt Brecht once said, "If cows could speak, there would be no slaughterhouses" (Pianca 134). I believe that if cows could speak, slaughterhouses would still exist, because there would be an ideology that would lead them where the ranchers want them to go. Slaughterhouses would not exist, however, if cows could speak and did not stop questioning the discourse, the religion of the ranchers. For them, then, there would be an alternative. How could there not be, then, an alternative for men and women who, in general, are more intelligent than cows?

VII. Success and Forgetting, Ethics and Memory

In *Time of Revenge* (Adolfo Aristaran, 1981) offers us an example of what we might call a "travesty of defeat," which reflects not only the concerns of Latin American art and filmography —noted at the beginning of this work—, but also of society as a whole. In the character portrayed by Federico Luppi —Bengoa—, we have a representative of the margin absorbed, in the classic style, by the center —a former unionist who seeks to erase, clean, sanitize his past to secure a position in a copper mine—. Of course, this center has relied on a despotic political power—the military dictatorship—, but it continues to act according to its best strategies: the persuasion of the correct discourse, the ethics of "free competition," of individual progress and of the Nation. However, this transformation of the personality in a man already graying cannot be sustained for long. And this premonition already appears as a warning from his father: "One day they will provoke you, and you will open your mouth," which also constitutes a symbolic key to the film: opening one's mouth to raise a voice of protest has until then brought more injustice, repression, and defeat. The margin cannot use the same strategies as the center, because the center does it better, its voice is stronger, and, worse still, it is more credible, more "centered," more "realistic," and "mature"7.

Time of Revenge culminates with a scene more symbolic than plausible, but necessary: the protagonist triumphs and utters a single word in the shower, in an intimate space: "we won." But after realizing that the enemy remains threatening—it has been offended but not destroyed—, he cuts out his tongue with the coldness of a surgeon. The tongue did not serve to save him but, on the contrary, ended up subjugating and enslaving him. As if that were not enough, his integration into the orbit of the ideological center had been thanks to his tongue. With it, he had lied and hidden his past. He had not needed it to defeat power, to vindicate himself as an ethical man, to honor his memory and justify his own existence, but through it, he could fall again. As his father said at the beginning, one day he would say what he shouldn't and would be lost again.

Time of Revenge is structured as a classic police genre film. However, we should not include it in the vast group composed of the reasonable, vulgar, and classic play of the Anglo-Saxon genre. Like so many other works of Latin American cinema, its epic consists of viewing its own society from the margins. Its flaws are often criticism, questioning, and a lack of understanding of the market. Its greatest

---

7 "I'm a little angel —says the old friend—. I don't protest. You have to eat. I play along. Don't speak, don't protest. This is hell."

virtue, perhaps, is having achieved a magnificent metaphor about the dialectic of power, a harsh and acerbic irony of class struggle.

From another perspective, and not from the tragedy of the dark years of the dictatorships but from the resignation of the integrated, we can consider *The Son of the Bride* (Juan José Campanella, 2001). Here the conflict between economic success and forgetfulness, between integration into modernity —or postmodernity— of consumerist capitalism or the inquisition of the guilty conscience that has forgotten, is expressed more explicitly. Perhaps Norma Aleandro represents Argentina: that immigrant past, almost romantic, beautiful, which has fallen ill with forgetfulness. At the same time, her son —the Argentinians— struggle to achieve recognition and do so through forgetfulness, without this mechanism being more effective than harmful.

The discourse of success, as Pianca calls it (120), was a deep mark in Argentina of the '90s, with its dream of already being in the "first world" —promise of President Carlos Saúl Menem—. It is necessary to forget in order to progress, to avoid conflict, the past. In The Son of the Bride, there is not only this conflict of memory-forgetfulness but also of tradition-modernity. Tradition —the family— is sprinkled with elements of North American life, such as the close-up shots of Burger King and Coca-Cola. The novelty of the first world is the image of progress that has been imposed by a dominant ideology, an ideology of success, and is, at the same time, forgetfulness as a prerequisite.

In the same way that we can understand forgetfulness or amnesia as a symptom of senile decay, we can also perceive, not the inability to remember but the will not to do so, as a typical trait of immaturity.

Perhaps it is in the character of the salesman —Roberto—, in *Minimal Stories* (Sorín, 2002) where the idea of being lost in a *labyrinth*: in a dialectical labyrinth, in a psychological labyrinth, in a physical labyrinth —the salesman has traveled more than two million kilometers—. Walking and traveling without stopping is no longer a form of knowledge, of memorization, but of forgetfulness. Like the compulsive work of the protagonist of *The Son of the Bride*, the endless journey to nowhere of the salesman in *Minimal Stories*, is an obsessive activity that anesthetizes, that prevents memory and awareness of our origin and our goals, as individuals and as a society. This is confirmed, at every moment, by his own self-destruction and the endless series of restarts—adaptation to new jobs, survival with new projects that are not carried out or are frustrated with the participation of their own author.

VIII. Tradition and nostalgia

In the case of *The Son of the Bride* there is an initial satire of the contemporary world represented, fundamentally, in the figure of Rafael (Ricardo Darín) and the already classic relationship of dependence and alienation that he maintains with his cell phone.

As it could not be otherwise, society filters into family and personal stories, but in this case it also does so consciously: the Argentine economic crisis, the corruption of public relations, etc.

However, the tradition of friendship and "the family" persists —and is the reason for that same conflict—, accentuated in the Río de la Plata (specifically Buenos Aires) by the Italian tradition. The characters belong to a typical Italian immigrant family.

But the crisis (or crossroads) is not only economic but also represents a change in personal relationships. The new ways of life seep into the old ones, often producing a negative change. In *The Son of the Bride* this change is represented by the stressful world of business that demands the son to live for and by his work, in contrast to the idyllic world of his father who, together with his mother, was able to start the restaurant and develop it in a romantic, rather than purely materialistic, way. Yet, the madness of the rat race is not enough. It barely allows him to avoid falling into the economic crisis and foreign competition, but at a very high cost: Rafael's health and the deterioration of his emotional relationships. These are not only represented in his inability to communicate with his partners and his daughter —who feels ignored—, but also in his relationship with his mother.

However, here another dimension of *The Son of the Bride* emerges, which transcends the protagonist's present: the emotional commerce with his mother, through affectionate gestures, has been equally unsatisfactory and, when it seemed to have been resolved by workaholism in pursuit of success, it reveals itself as immutable, like a pending debt that, due to his mother's illness, seems impossible to pay.

The Son of the Bride begins with a scene that we know —through its narrative and photographic technique, its costumes, and intuition— belongs to the childhood of one of the protagonists. Children playing with an old ball, in a marginal, destroyed setting, almost a cemetery, wearing jerseys of Buenos Aires football clubs, Boca and River, develop a "small" childish power struggle. It is the moment when the *Fox* (Rafael Belverdere, in his childhood) appears with a slingshot to deliver justice8. This, like many other scenes in the film, is classic: the righteous child will become something else, but he will never forget his ideal past and will make sure to translate and repeat it as a legitimization of his future actions. When he becomes a gastronomic entrepreneur, he will remind his father —or, rather, put into his father's mouth— that he taught him to fight for "ideals." To which his father (Héctor Alterio) will deny it using parody and humor.

---

[8] It could be intentional that El Zorro wears the Boca Juniors jersey —as a representative of the popular— and is pursued by his classic sporting and neighborhood rival, River Plate, —the 'millionaires.'"

After the nostalgic images of childhood —a trademark of the Río de la Plata, of the philosophy of tango, the protective affection of "the grandmother"— the present bursts in with all its madness —also archetypal—: the same blue-eyed owner eats hurriedly, while working, giving orders, and talking on his cell phone at all times and in any place9. Emphasizing this image of postmodern alienation, the cell phone is erased from the image through the use of a microphone and earpiece (which allows talking without stopping "working"), reinforcing a pathetic image: the new worker, the entrepreneur talks to himself, he is as alienated as his mother. Or more —as will be suggested in many parts of the film.

When the three return to the nursing home, the mother says: "I won't leave your father here." After entering, her image will overlap with the image of her son's face reflected in the glass door, which implies a questioning: it is not clear if it is "logical" for the mother to be there or with her family, but at all times the blame is placed on "that illness" that her mother suffers from: *the loss of memory*, which prevents her from living among others.

The celebration of the mother's birthday is done by the son and the father in the absence of the honoree, who still

---

9The elderly couple in love is alternatively shown with their son in the background, talking frantically on his cell phone. The calm and understanding words of the father contrast with the son's lack of comprehension and his vocabulary full of insults and outbursts.

lives in the same city. This significant absence is multi-significant: the mother is a disappeared person—she is neither alive nor dead—in some way, she is the past that has gone. Both toast with the best champagne while looking at an absence, saying: "Happy birthday, mommy." But, at the same time, the celebration is absurd, it lacks the subject, those who organized it have lost the sense of the ceremony, not because of the mother's dementia but their own, which will be reversed, in part, towards the end, which begins to take shape at this very moment.

The protagonist, Rafael, will make his emotional conflicts explicit. The breakdown of the relationship with his mother—the mother, the protective grandmother—as a result of his disobedience—having abandoned his law career—will leave a deep mark on him, on the son who is unrecognized, unaccepted by his mother. But the son will try desperately to prove to her that he is "not useless," even though he didn't become *my son the doctor*." It will be of no use for his father to question this interpretation ingrained in his conscious-unconscious: "Who told you that you were the useless one in the family?"

In this case, Rafael's conflict will be, above all, selfish but understandable: he needs his mother to recognize his worth, but she can no longer do so. Nevertheless, he insists on obtaining a sign of this recognition and what he gets is a confession: his mother also suffered the "lack of love" from her own mother.

32

Now, how is Rafael supposed to have sought to overcome this conflict, this lack of maternal recognition? Through obsessive work. An activity that not only prevented him from stopping to think—the desire and belief that he had to be involved in every detail of his business—but also brought him success: "I've done much better than several professionals I know," says Rafael, which is not only a social reality in Argentina, but also a goal of the character who needs to compare himself to what he considers most important (a result of the maternal model). Now, in this desperate race to prove that professional success, which supposedly would compensate for the lack, the protagonist needs to be alone. Others and their affections represent an obstacle in his competitive career. This is not only reflected in his relationship with his ex-wife but with everyone else. He proposes "more freedom" to his girlfriend, even though he loves her, and warns his daughter: "Don't be a pain in the neck, I can't divorce you."

To maintain this mechanical order, even family relationships, fragmented by separations, divorces, misunderstandings, and new unions, must be structured like business: "Today is Thursday—says the daughter—; it's my turn with dad." Immediately after, and following a custody dispute, the father takes her away in a hurry, with the same urgency he applies to his professional matters.

But the heart attack must serve as a dramatic wake-up call. It will mark a turning point in his life, which becomes evident as soon as he wakes up in the hospital bed. Then he realizes that one of his dreams is "to get the hell out of here."

That is his initial solution: faced with the unresolved conflict, he flees —a will to forget. Obsessive work was also a form of escape, which is why it is not at this moment that he redirects his life. Going to Mexico to raise horses is more of a change in form than in content.

However, I believe that the most important symbolism in *The Son of the Bride*—and the one that structures an underlying plot—is the one referring to the saga of *Zorro* 10, the avenger. He will appear repeatedly, starting from the children's game at the beginning, then in the adult world, with frequent allusions to each character —like Sergeant García, etc.—, or in the movies that Rafael will watch alone during his moments of existential crisis.

Zorro is an avenger and, like all archetypes of the era, he is a loner—like The Lone Ranger, etc.—. For this archetype, success and justice depend on a single man and, as if that weren't enough, it is possible.

Only the friend will turn to this story to contradict the positivist discourse of the childhood hero: "The fourteen-year-olds are still messing with the eight-year-olds." But Sergeant García has discovered the sad truth and, moreover, has been defeated.

---

10 A popular American series among Río de la Plata children during the 60s and 70s.

IX. Strategies of Domination and Resistance

For Zavarzaeh, the relationship between the center and the margin is one of oppositions, conflictual, between exclusion and inclusion. Its crisis is one of the symptoms of Postmodernity —"[The] relation between the center and the margin [...] is itself a symptom of the crisis of postmodernity and uncertainty about the norms that might 'justify' and 'explain' the acts one undertakes." (169)

However, what exactly does the "crisis" of the traditional relationship between the center and the margin mean? Undoubtedly, this relationship has not changed since the Neolithic era: there is a center from which a dominant discourse is emitted, which is, at the same time, exclusionary. Those who are harmed by this discourse or those who resist it must, necessarily, position themselves on the margins. The crisis of this dialectical relationship means, above all, a consciousness and an ethical questioning of this relationship, long before any structural —spatial— change of the traditional center.

Now, how does the center dominate, and how does the margin defend itself? How does the margin react, and how does the center reorganize itself?

It is important to note that the center is the main producer of "legitimations," that is, the primary author of the dominant ethical discourse. But this discourse needs an enemy: the margin. Personally, I believe that one of the strengths of the center in relation to the "res intermedia" lies in maintaining a clear ethical-symbolic relationship with the margin. In other words, the center needs the margin. Without danger and threat, effective ideological domination could not exist. It is for this reason that the center must combat the ethical-contestatory emergence of the margin but never completely suppress it. If the margin did not exist, the center would invent it. This perverse relationship, which feeds on antagonisms, has been a characteristic of almost all of Latin America. Its legacy has even been transmitted invisibly but powerfully to "democracies" like Uruguay or Argentina.

A second form of "ideological manipulation" practiced by the center, apart from antagonism, is "absorption." What we could also call "integration of exclusion" or "nullification of dissent[11]" (Zavarzaeh 178).

What remains unclear is whether the center is plural or not. We know that the margin is, but the answer is not so clear when we interrogate the center. There are two possibilities: a) the center is singular, by ideological nature and hierarchical organization; or b) the center is a "coherent" plurality, that is, capable of integrating the different levels and categories of domination discourses: racial, class, economic, gender, etc.—a woman of the dominant class

---

[11][Hollywood films] attempt to recuperate the radical margin as a "reformist" discourse. The margin and its discourses, in a gesture of open-mindedness, are seen as having a "positive" effect on the center." Op. Cit. p. 170. "[In Desperately Seeking Susan] margin that can form a moral coalition with the center" (178)

would, in some way and at the same time, be marginal due to her sex.

We know that a fundamental part of the dominant ideology, the "central" ideology, consists of associating the margin with ethical disqualifiers, such as those of social, sexual, or productive order. That is, the margin is unproductive, disorderly, dangerous to order and security, sexually deviant or unnatural, immature, etc.

In Hollywood films, the margin ultimately integrates into the center—the hippie, the bohemian, the dissenter, the "libertine" woman, etc., end up failing or integrating into the capitalist structure. At times, the margin appears as an innocent form that will fulfill a "reformist" function for some dysfunctional elements of the center—to which it must help recover its own centrality in times of "deviation." At other times, the margin appears recognizing itself as incapable of serious changes and as a characteristic of the psychological, ideological, productive, and moral immaturity of the society it criticizes.

On the contrary, in Latin American films like *The Crime of Father Amaro* the center ultimately triumphs in the plot, but this triumph signifies a necessary ethical defeat in the meta-plot, that is, in the probable readings of the viewer. The center is revealed, this time, as immoral, corrupt. This film also presents a paradox that, though it may surprise, is not at all a property of postmodernity but of the origins of Christianity: the center represents social force and power, domination, at the same time as ethical marginality. From this perspective, this discourse is marginal. Only the power of the dominant can impose censorship of expression; but the censor is, historically, the one who has lost the battle for ethical legitimation, because their discourse is insufficient. The character of Father Natalio represents the typical marginalized figure: he is in political and ecclesiastical clandestinity. He is also marginalized by political, civil power, represented by the town's newspaper. Yet, he is the only "ethical hero" who survives the ethical annihilation of the film. His defeat, the excommunication—the definitive separation from corruption and power— like that of Jesus, is the only effective form of moral triumph.

As stated by Mas'ud Zavarzaeh, a professor at the University of Berkeley, dissent is part of the tradition of current systems of domination. Tradition integrates and resolves two fundamental topics of capitalist societies: the new and the permanent. To do this, tradition resorts to the "de-historization" of social and political events. It integrates the "dissenter," the rebel, into its own discourse as necessary results of a dynamic, modern, and pluralistic—democratic society.

But this "de-historization" is a dramatic and paradoxical form of forgetting through memory, a *memorization of forgetting*: the ingestion of historical facts by an ideologized tradition.

In the case of Latin America, the rebel, the subversive, when they failed in a great revolutionary movement to destroy the structure of social domination —which is the general rule—, ended up integrating into an even more perverse tradition: they operated as justification for the despotic domination of political, religious, and military powers.

X. In the search for a functional resistance

Zuzana M. Pick, recalling the times of political militancy in the 1960s, pointed out: "As I have written elsewhere, the films of the movement called for 'direct political action: denouncing injustice, misery and exploitation, analyzing [their] causes and consequences, replacing humanism by violence'" (Pick 302).

In the perpetual search for change, the strategies and proposals were diverse. In line with the 1960s, this response often leaned toward violent forms. Glauber Rocha defined it as follows: *"The most noble cultural manifestation of hunger is violence" "It is the initial moment when the colonizer became aware of the colonized"* (Rocha 60)

We can observe a change and conjecture an explanation: after the Latin American dictatorships of the 1970s and 1980s, the call for violent action as a way to provoke change —the eternal change that never comes— has given way to a more "humanist" —or simply moderate?— search for the same change. *"This discourse of 'present-ness' is crucial to many of the films of New Latin American Cinema"* Directors and filmmakers have consciously taken on a leading role as agents of social change. *"Their films served to make ideological positions explicit and to intervene ideologically in favor of social change through aesthetic strategies (...)"* (304)

Consistent with its obsessive search for change, overwhelmed by an always adverse present, Latin American art has also obsessively sought to be an agent of change. Unlike the Hollywood criterion, where the social order is not in question, where, on the contrary, the effort must focus on maintaining it rather than modifying it. Both Latin American literature and cinema have sought change, sometimes through the exposure of an unjust reality, sometimes through alternative discourse. It is what the Argentine filmmaker Fernando Birri, referring to the cinema of recent decades, called an attempt at "a poetics of transformation of reality." (93)

Although with greater skepticism, in the 1990s Latin American art has sought the transformation of society but no longer through the sacrifice of the individual but, precisely, by reclaiming it. Reclaiming it from the abstract discourses of traditional leftist ideologies and the call of the dominant ideology —the capitalist one— for a renunciation of their present claims in the hope of a future achievement that never arrives.

XI. The loss of collective memory

While we will find an intermediate tradition where memory becomes denunciation, the rewriting of forgotten history, we will also have a "documentary" genre, in the broad sense of the word, where the present is captured and turned into future memory, as in the cases of *La vendedora de rosas* and *La virgen de los sicarios*.

Within the first group, we could place, as examples, *La Historia oficial* (Argentina, 1983), Amanecer Rojo (Mexico, 1989), Botín de Guerra (Argentina 1999), Kamchatka (Argentina 2002). In all of them, the discourse is one of denunciation against "the official history," against the history written by power, whether state, religious, or economic. The main motivation for this rewriting is political and, in all cases, consists of a struggle for the recovery of memory, not only the memory hidden by power but also that which has been distorted by it.

If at the beginning, referring to the revolutionary years of the '60s, we said that *there is no consciousness without memory*, now we must say that *without memory there is no truth*.

A third stage in this *via crucis* of Latin American memory is the loss of *collective memory*, which, paradoxically, will become a future document: a memory of forgetting.

In this stage, we will mention two examples, such as *La virgen de los sicarios* and *La vendedora de rosas*. Both, from

41

different approaches, challenge the traditional structure of Hollywood cinema and reverse the precept of art as a means of entertainment or beauty, of art as an aesthetic object, purely —if such a puritanical form of art without ethical implications ever truly existed—. Both films not only seek to expose a dramatic reality known to many, but they will one day be the best documentary source for those who seek to understand something about our present, specifically the present of the marginalized societies of Latin America.

However, here we no longer have denunciation with the aim of rewriting history. The goal is no longer to "recover" a lost memory, but to expose the tragedy of the most devastating and absolute forgetting. It has much less to do with the memory of Utopia. Here, not only is there no pursuit of the perfect society, but there is not even an attempt at resistance from a defeated society: a deep and dark nihilism, sometimes self-indulgent, runs through these cinematic proposals. A violent concordance with reality, the degradation of life, death —forgetting. Here, the present contrasts violently and points us to the science-fiction-catastrophe genre, where the world has succumbed to chaos and people—a submerged class, far from the powerful, as always—desperately seek to survive amidst the worst misery and abandonment, amidst violence and alienation. La vendedora de rosas tells us that this future has already arrived, that chaos is now, that the world is already lost. Destruction, moral and material—decay—coexist with elements of modernity, with symbols of a distant developed world, with the fragmented memory of objects that were once useful, that once formed part of an order full of memory. Only here, unlike Hollywood, there are no promises of redemption, no heroes organizing resistance, incubating rebellion. There is no hope, only death. Death to achieve virginal liberation; death —as it actually happens— to return to the arms of the mother.

For the characters of *La vendedora de Rosas*, the symbols—the collective memory—have lost their meaning; the text, its memory. The fact of the "loss of collective memory" is accentuated not only by drugs —that erase everything—, but also by the age of its protagonists —children— and by the poverty of language, which is, in sum, collective memory.

There is no fiction, in the traditional sense of the term; the actors are not professionals, and their role is to represent themselves. Or, even more, they do not represent anything but continue their lives as if the camera were not present. This is no longer the neorealism born in the poor neighborhoods of Italy and Latin America: it is raw *hyperrealism*, human waste—supposedly still alive —excreted into the sewers of the modern city.

Paradoxically, just as the bones of a primitive man today serve to remind the rest of the men and women who surrounded him, without any of them ever intending it, so will these memories of forgetting serve to remind us of what we once were —if one day we are lucky enough to stop being *that* which we also are.

Bibliography

Blacker, Irwing R. The elements of Screenwriting, Macmillan, New York, 1996.

Cook, David A. *A history of Narrative Film*, David. W.W. Norton & Company, Inc.

Cuadernos de Cine Número 33. *El nuevo cine Latinoamericano en el mundo de hoy. Memorias del IX Festival Internacional del Nuevo Cine Latinoamericano.* Universidad Autónoma de México. México, 1988.

El crimen del padre Amaro. (México, 2002) Dirección: Carlos Carrera. Producción: Alfredo y Daniel Ripstein.

El hijo de la novia. Argentina, 2001. Dir. Juan José Campanella. Perf. Ricardo Darín, Norma Aleandro.

Gómez-Tarín, Francisco Javier. *Cine y revolución en Latinoamérica.* IV Jornadas de Lenguas y Culturas Amerindias.

Historias mínimas. Argentina 2002. Dir. Carlos Sorín.

Kamchatka. Argentina, 2002. Dir: Piñeiro. Perf. Ricardo Darín.

La historia oficial. Argentina 1984. Perf. Norma Aleandro

La hora de los hornos. Argentina, Solanas y Getino, 1968.

La vendedora de rosas. Colombia, 1998. Dirección: Gaviria.

La virgen de los sicarios. Colombia. Guión: Fernando Vallejo. Director: Barbet Schroeder.

Memorias del subdesarrollo. Dir. Tomas Gutiérrez Alea, Cuba 1968

Pianca, Marina. La política de la dislocación (o retorno a la memoria del futuro), en Memoria colectiva y Políticas del olvido, Argentina y Uruguay, 1970-1990. Beatriz Viterbo Editora, Buenos Aires, 1997.

Pick, Zuzana M. The New Latin America Cinema/ A modernist Critique of Modernity. En New Latin America Cinema, Edited by Michael T. Martin, Wayne State University Press, Detroit, 1997.

Pick, Zuzana M., The New Latin America Cinema/ A modernist Critique of Modernity. En New Latin America Cinema, Edited by Michael T. Martin, Wayne State University Press, Detroit, 1997.

Rocha, Glauber, An Esthetic of Hunger. *The New Latin America Cinema/ A modernist Critique of Modernity*. En *New Latin America Cinema*, Edited by Michael T. Martin, Wayne State University Press, Detroit, 1997.

Selles Gómes, Paulo Emílio, "Cinema: A Trajectory within underdevelopment", Austin: University of Texas Press, 1988.

Stam, Robert, Burgoyne, Robert, Flitterman-Lewins Sandy Nuevos conceptos de la teoría del cine. Ed. Piados 1999. Página 215.

Tiempo de revancha. Dirección: Adolfo Aristaran. Guión: Emilio Kauderer. 1981

Zavarzaeh, Mas'ud, Seeing Films Politically, pg. 169. State University of New York Press, Albany, 1991.

EL MÉGANO

García Espinosa-Tomas Gutiérrez Alea, 1956

We can say that *El mégano* is a "revolutionary" film in a triple aspect: technical, thematic, and ideological. We know that years later Julio García Espinosa would theorize about the techniques of revolutionary cinema as an "imperfect cinema", probably as a consequence of prior study and practice in the aesthetics of Italian neorealism from his time at the Centro Sperimentale di Roma, so present in this film. According to Chanan,

Julio García Espinosa [...] put forward a powerful apologia for this experimental effervescence in his manifesto of 1968, *Por un cine imperfecto* (For an imperfect cinema) in which he argued that the imperfections of a low budget cinema of urgency, which sought to create a dialog with its audience, were preferable to the sheen of high production values that merely reflected the audience back to itself" (6).

We can think that this "imperfection" is due not only to the scarcity of technological means of production and execution[12] but also to the will to challenge a "perfect

---

[12] Chanan describes the difficulties the Revolution itself faced, years later, in obtaining technical equipment abroad (Che in Japan, etc.) and especially when the period of nationalization of American companies began, followed by the embargo against the island: "ICAIC was able to acquire several crucial pieces of equipment: a Mitchell camera, an optical camera

cinema" represented by the Hollywood film industry. The first point is fulfilled in *El mégano*: it does not seem that technical resources and a large budget accompanied its production. It is no coincidence that Italian neorealism chose the poor classes to create its art, but for Cuban revolutionary cinema, "neorealism" overflowed this aesthetic and ideological choice to embody itself in the very process of filming. In *El mégano*, some "sloppiness" seems to have occurred in some sequence changes regarding sound, although the very idea of "sloppiness" may be conditioned by an aesthetic and "semantic" sensibility developed within the same consumption habits formed by Hollywood and commercial cinema.[13] It has not been the Brechtian precept that has prevailed in commercial cinema throughout the 20th century: "imperfection" could function as an interruptor of hypnotic daydreaming, something with which a revolutionary (or at least a rebel) like Bertolt Brecht might have agreed. Also, the initial slowness, as oppressive as the work in the mégano itself, far from the dynamics of commercial cinema, which always feels compelled to tell a story quickly and intriguingly, overloaded—especially in our era

---

(for special effect works), an animation table, and laboratory equipment, all from the United States." (129)

[13] Alfredo Guevara conducted a survey of the films being watched in Cuba in 1989. The overwhelming majority were Hollywood films. His conclusion was that "[a]verage taste has been maltreated and certain overridden influences have created 'habits' of cinema difficult to eradicate... the genres together with the star system predominate and their formulas amount to anticinema." (Chanan, 137).

of late capitalism—with a great overstimulation of signs and special effects.

Despite all that has been noted before, we can think that not even the creators of *El mégano* could escape the aesthetic and semiotic codes that characterized Hollywood cinema for so many years. In this sense, the second point (about the will to challenge the codes of hegemonic cinema) falls a bit short. This can be seen mainly in the dramatization of the story through the music, which is even of the same type as that used in old *far west* films and American suspense films: oboes and violins that constantly indicate what the emotional state of the viewer should be: tension, action, relaxation, surprise, intrigue, etc.

The title of the film is not accidental, nor is the choice of this type of work, and not, for example, work in the sugarcane fields (a symbol of Cuba, since the time of José Martí). The mangrove has a strong metaphorical as well as psychological charge: its characters, the "real" men and women, are submerged, struggling with an invisible reality, with the rescue of decay or the fossilization of the trunks to survive. On the other hand, they are not traditional farmers: they are wage earners, a kind of pre-industrial proletariat.

But the symbolism is not limited to the title; at least three or four images have this function. (1) The girl, Paulita, dirtying her doll's face in the image and likeness of her parents' faces. The parallel is probable: the girl and her doll are to the wage earners of the mangrove as the producers

48

and the film are to Cuban spectators before the revolution. (2) The woman repeatedly placing herself at the door of the hut would acquire parodic dimensions if it were not a drama, so we can think of a critique of the "old patriarchal order" (later confirmed in *Manuela* and forgotten years later in the post-revolutionary rhetoric that provoked, as a reaction, a film like *Fresa y Chocolate*). (3) The difference in the *whites* of the shirts of the exploited contrasting with the neat shirts of the exploiters, the dirty faces of the women of the mangrove and the "painted little mouths" of the women of the idle employer class establishes a visual, symbolic, and class difference, where the "villain" is no longer the unscrupulous rogue, inhabitant of the *villas*, but the "noble" inhabitant of the neat castles. (3) Finally, the protagonist's fist at the end (shown in close-up as the final *message*) not only represents rebellion but also the Communist Party itself.

The ending, from a narrative point of view, is open— we do not know what will happen next, the conflict has not been resolved but merely posed. From a thematic point of view, it is closed: there is no longer room for Resignation but for Revolution.

MEMORIES OF UNDER-DEVELOPMENT

Tomas Gutiérrez Alea, Cuba 1968

"In underdevelopment, nothing has continuity, everything is forgotten. Now begins your final destruction."
Sergio, main character of *Memories of Underdevelopment*

As the sixties draw to a close, the most important revolution in Cuban history approaches its tenth anniversary. From the unquestionable overthrow of a personalist tyranny (1959) to the complex—and at least seemingly impossible—project of building a utopia, long dreamed of by Europe and later by the "virgin continent": the utopia of a just society, whose organization would be based on reason, dialectics, and history. It is at this moment that the relationship between the individual and society enters a crisis and is redefined.

At the time *Memories of Underdevelopment* is filmed, the Cuban and Cuban society are taking stock. An anniversary with a zero at the end forces a reckoning with the achievements and results of the commemorated event. A part of this Cuban society does not participate in the Grand Collective Project (for political reasons or reasons of individual interest), and many of them leave the country. But each of them is not simply a political adversary of those who decide to remain in their homeland: each of them are friends, brothers, wives, mothers, or lovers.

It is more or less at this moment that *Memories of Underdevelopment* begins. Scenes of farewells, explicit signs ("people are leaving the country"), or the subtle and ironic whistle of Sergio, the protagonist (if Adelita were to leave with another) confirm the importance of this theme: desertion, abandonment, or exile, which is the harshest form of questioning the Revolution. And then the inevitable question: are the exiles victims or traitors?

From the beginning of the film, the need is evident, on the part of its creators, to maintain a certain critical distance, both from the revolution and from the "deserters." In fact, this is almost a necessary condition of all art and all true reflection, whether literary or philosophical. However, this need will not be entirely satisfied by the facts of the *cinematic discourse*—if I may use the expression—: the "deserters" are presented, almost unequivocally, as petty individuals, with personal and bourgeois interests, in a permanent search for justification to legitimize their voluntary exile (the clearest cases are Sergio's wife and his friend).

The strategies of *Memories of Underdevelopment* to organize its cinematic discourse are diverse: from direct symbolism (the cage and the bird; repetitive interrogatives like Sergio's yawn, etc.) to almost documentary exposition (such as the data comparing the number of deaths in World War II and those caused by disease and hunger in Latin America), passing through philosophical reflection (ethical reflections on individual and collective behavior, the torturer during Batista's time who justifies himself and hides behind the group, etc.) and the author's interior monologue, supported by images, sometimes with humor (an interior monologue that, moreover, is the main voice, the alter ego of Desnoes, Gutiérrez Alea and, probably, of an entire intellectual community of the time).

Additionally, several technical experiments are evident, such as the replacement of Sergio's eyes with the filming camera for a long period of time; several introspective gazes, not only at society, which is contrasted in its hypocrisy by antagonistic images (a dead body, an aristocrat applauding elegantly, etc.), but also at the film itself: direct criticism of repetitive entertainment cinema (shaping the subject) in which everything is stupidly repeated; criticism of the inconsistent character of Hollywood women, later repeated in Elena-*subject*, etc. A criticism that also extends to an icon of the 20th century: Hemingway ("Cuba never interested him" "It was his tropical refuge"

There is also an introspective look at the cinematic act itself, expressed in the intention, on the part of the protagonists of ICAIC, to make a collage film using those scenes censored by Batista's regime.

But from the critique of cinema itself, as a producer of sensibilities and ideology (of subjects), the film places greater emphasis on a search for the definition of *underdevelopment*, both national and individual, as if one were explanatory of the other (or they were the same thing), and seeks in this the explanation for a possible triumph or failure of Utopia.

Regarding the latter, we could point to several scenes, but for the sake of brevity, I prefer to focus on one in particular, which, while it may not be central to the cinematic discourse, is at least revealing. Or it has been for me.

After portraying the psychology of Elena (or Helena: Hellenic, the decadent character of the Greek, the loss of the Dionysian) over several scenes, Gutiérrez Alea resorts to the direct reflection of the protagonist, Sergio, to finally explain, in an extremely direct manner, what had been sensed long before: Elena is Latin America, that inconstant, unstable woman who never matures in her character. As we see a summary of her physical attitudes, her gestures, Sergio laments her lack of consequence, consistency, her inability to accumulate experience. Cubans—Latin Americans—adapt to the moment. Elena is the image of underdevelopment (the opposite of Hannah, the German woman who flees the Nazi regime): she is incapable of sustaining a feeling, and in this idea, there is a strong whiff of Nietzschean ink, of his recurrence of the will, of character, of instinct as a state of maturity.

In *Memories of Underdevelopment* there are, at times, reflections on the causes of underdevelopment in a very direct way, but also on the social, economic, cultural, and psychological contradictions that implicitly predict the idea of failure, if not social, at least individual (existential: reflections of Sartrean absurdity appear especially at the end, though at the beginning there are already questions like Sergio's: "What is the meaning of life for me, for them?"). There is a strong burden of doubts and uncertainties: Will we be capable? Will the Grand

Collective Project make sense in this current sociocultural state (of immaturity)?

These reflections, of course, are not entirely canonical from a materialist point of view (let us remember that Marx himself was surprised by certain cultural permanences when the relations of production had disappeared thousands of years ago): the infrastructure has changed (the relations of production), but the superstructure has not. The character of the people has not reached maturity. In fact, it resists. In the trial for sexual abuse by Elena and her family, Sergio is acquitted by formal justice, but he has emerged defeated from his experience with Elena's family (the people), which has shown all the strength of cultural rigidity. "I have seen too much to be innocent," reflects the protagonist; "they have too much darkness in their heads to be guilty."

But the abyss does not only separate Sergio from his lovers, his friends. It also separates him from his mother, who repeatedly sends him things he does not need. "We don't manage to understand each other." "I can't read the old woman's handwriting," he says. On the other hand, the abyss does not leave Sergio on the better side: "I am 38 years old, and I don't feel wiser or more mature." "In the tropics, everything matures and decomposes easily; nothing persists," he reiterates the idea of immaturity several times ("Hannah was a mature woman, different from the girls here") and, at the same time, the loss of youth: women go from youth to decay. He too arrives "too early or too late."

If at the beginning *Memories of Underdevelopment* threatens the viewer with subjecting them to ninety minutes of a pamphlet-like and officialist discourse, it immediately reveals a synthesizing wisdom that is deeply unsettling, which is characteristic of great works of art, since the time of the Greek classics: upon leaving the projection room (the theater), the viewer is no longer who they were. A revelation has taken place in the witness. Even more, Memories of Underdevelopment is capable—in a rather daring way—of surprising us with direct conclusions we would expect to find in an analytical poet. (In fact, there is more than one similarity with Dostoevsky's Notes from Underground, aside from the title.)

To what extent is *Memories of Underdevelopment* an "officialist" film, and to what extent is it subversive or inquisitive? To answer this question, we must not forget the regional scale we are referring to. That is, we must not forget that even an officialist discourse in Cuba is, when extending the boundaries slightly beyond the natural limits of the island, always a form of response to the dominant discourse; a form of "subaltern culture" in opposition to the "predominant culture" of capitalist Western society.

The ending is one of waiting. Not only is a political outcome expected (a new invasion by the United States, as a consequence of the Missile Crisis), which could mean war (and for which the people are not entirely aware, as if it were a game), but it is also a waiting that is, at the same time, the time that separates an existential question of transcendental importance from the answer, which will likely never come.

DEATH OF A BUREAUCRAT

Tomás Gutiérrez Alea (1966)

I believe we could all agree that Death of a Bureaucrat is a satire or a parody. Like all satires or parodies, it is a caricature with strong critical content, where the predominant features are absurdity, contradiction, and mockery.

Surely, we will not agree on the object of this biting critique. The title seems to hint at the answer: it is a parody of bureaucracy. In fact, if we refer to the text itself—in this case, the film—we could say the same: the fact that the action takes place in any country on the planet is circumstantial, as "the evil of bureaucracy" can be considered universal from the times of Hammurabi to George W. Bush, passing, naturally, through Franz Kafka.

However, any analysis, no matter how minimal, must consider the context of the work and its creators. It could also be argued that considering the context should not mean nullifying the "meta-contextual" values, that is, the universal ones. In other words, we could consider this film, like any work of art, as a creative reflection on the human condition. This is undeniable.

Nevertheless, let us keep one detail in mind: Cuba. Every context is, by definition, a particular constellation of texts. Applied to the problem of cinema, Mas'ud Zavarzaeh understands it this way, incorporating the concept of "tale":

The tale in the film is not in the text itself (is not a positive entity): it is not determined. Therefore, is not accessible through an analysis of formal properties [from inside a film itself][14]. (18)

And in revolutionary Cuba, it is not possible to abstract oneself from those texts that, ubiquitously, include a predominant and sometimes overwhelming political and ideological factor for any other human perspective. One is born politically, makes love politically, and dies politically. This no longer means a way of seeing reality but reality itself. Minna Jaskari quotes Michael Chanan on the same idea: "Cuban cinema is synonymous with the Cuban Revolution." (Jaskari)

Let us first look at these satirical elements that find in the image of cinema an especially fertile ground.

The idea of the title alludes, first and foremost, to a dead person. And a dead person is what we will have as the central protagonist throughout the entire story. Soon we will discover that this is not the dead person the title refers to, as the central dead person was not a bureaucrat but an "artist" (we will see later the sarcasm of this term). Therefore, we already have the suspense assured: the filmic text will culminate with

---

[14] "But each film is also the narrative space of contestation and struggle among different tales" (19) [...] A filmic space is the site of warring forces in culture between what social reality is under present ideological and economic practices and what it could become. (23) [...] One way to allow other tales to surface is to use the device of renarrating to displace the overt tale." (25)

the death of one of the secondary characters, justly, judging by the implicit plot that will make the viewer hate each of these officials.[15]

The satire leaves no element unused: from the beginning, the credits of the film itself are presented with the elements of a state office in any country in the world in the 1960s. The symbol, a typewriter. The repeated headings of "Whereas" and "Inasmuch" speak of a routine that has nothing revolutionary about it (at first) while the stamp (or seal) "Ask González" reminds us of our own experiences close to the power of the bureau. (This same attitude will be developed later in the film more explicitly). At the same time, as the typewriter strikes like an army, the reason for all bureaucratic logic cannot be missing: not the population, the State, the Homeland, present in the music of the national anthem. Finally, the dedication is also a parody or, at least, laden with sarcasm: "Dedicate this film to Luis Buñuel." This can well be understood as "dedicated to the master of surrealism," not for an aesthetic reason but for a practical one: the events depicted reflect a surreal, absurd reality. We can think that dedicating it to Luis Buñuel was because the Spaniard was a filmmaker, like Alea, and is recognized by the public as a surrealist. But it could also have been dedicated to Franz Kafka, if the Cuban public had had more literary than

---

[15] The burial of the bureaucrat, in the final image, reminded me, by its tone of parody, of the celebrations of 'the burial of the sardine' in Spain. The music and solemnity are the same. The absurd, Goyian.

cinematic culture. The crossed-out name is no less significant. Someone was there in the dedication before censorship (the repression, let's say psychoanalytic) removed that name. If it weren't for the fact that Gutiérrez Alea was not anti-Castro, one might say that the crossed-out name was in place of the name of the Caudillo, after all the primary responsible for that "permanence" in Cuban civilian life.

Of course, the sound of a toilet flushing that follows the credits is a too direct indication. After all, it is not only a critique of Cuban bureaucracy but also humor[16]. Or, if not, humor has been used for critique, as a form of apology.

The voiceover at the beginning, verbose, is another element we can associate with Fidel Castro. The convoluted explanation of the doctor, the pseudo-intellectual, the deskbound charlatan with a bust of Socrates in the background reiterates this dialectical labyrinth that resembles the labyrinth of papers, exaggeratedly carried by machines and trucks (which increases, by contrast, by absence, the sense of "useless effort, of unproductivity). The reference to the history of the pharaohs, while it may have a connection to a dead person buried with a personal object, demonstrates a kind of autism in the discourse, further accentuated by the

---

[16] The fact that it is the nephew of the deceased and not his own son who undergoes the ordeal of exhuming him demonstrates, in my opinion, that Alea had no intention of dramatizing the film but quite the opposite. The nephew only rebels twice: the first time, almost at the end, tired, he says not without humor: "Oh my mother, this is death"; the second is the most obvious moment.

lawyer's concern with the buttocks of the women around him. And what is bureaucracy if not state autism?

Another filmmaker could have shared the dedication with Luis Buñuel, if the central theme had not been so much a critique of Cuban bureaucratic absurdity but a critique of modernity: Charles Chaplin. It is not necessary to note that the scene of the sculpture-producing machine is a direct allusion to Modern Times: the movements of silent cinema, the rebellion of the machine, the very act of the human inserting themselves into it, the machine itself, etc.17 A new element is added to the allusion of modern man due to the mechanization of his world: the alienation of attempting to produce art in a standardized way, to produce José Martí as one produces soap or car parts.18 But Death of a Bureaucrat is not Modern Times and, therefore, its critique does not focus on the mechanist alienation of the West but on something more localized: Cuba, the Cuban Revolution. "Comrades, comrades" is repeated like the busts of José Martí. From the singularity of the artistic and revolutionary act, we begin to move to the empty routine of repeated discourse, the standardization of art, and, perhaps worse: the

---

17 Another allusion to *Modern Times* is when the protagonist flees with a trash can and is chased by people in the street until they catch him. Here, what Mas'ud Zavarzaeh would call a "reparation" of the rebel is put into motion.
18 The industrial reproduction of José Martí's busts signifies the repetition of a discourse. Moreover, this "industrialization" of "art" reminds us of the paradoxical expression canonically associated with Hollywood: "the film industry" (not to mention "the Mecca of cinema...")

propagandistic manipulation of art. This is evidenced by another satire among this accumulation of satires: the artist's workshop (factory) has become an advertising agency in favor of the revolution and against an "imperialism" that begins to be confused with the discourse, with the necessary enemy, which is not even advertising for export but for internal consumption. I am sure that Gutiérrez Alea must have despised the conception of art as declared by the "socialist realists" of Stalin's time. And the abuse of advertising, of ideological pamphlets, of banal allegory, of the manipulation of art must have meant for him and his group as dangerous as bureaucracy itself19. For its part, Death of a Bureaucrat gathers a collection of incomplete posters and background elements that force us to read between the lines ("Eradicate ...ism," etc.) and other intertextualities like the elevator operator singing *E lucevan le stelle* by Puccini. Other allusions to American cinema are evident. The humor of confusion ("Who lives?" asks the cemetery watchman) and physical humor (the fights at the cemetery entrance, with meringue pies, where the police are always among the victims) clearly reference The Three Stooges; the car losing its doors and fenders is a clear allusion to Laurel and Hardy. The music, moreover, enhances this cocktail by paying "homage" to the circus. In an inverse sense, I believe that *Esperando la carroza*

---

[19] Observe the repetition of clenched fists in the pamphlets. From the clenched fist of El Mégano to these clenched fists, symbols of the Party, much water has flowed under the bridge.

(Langsner, 1974; film version with Gasalla) must have been inspired by *Muerte de un burócrata*.[20]

Minna Jaskari understands *La muerte de un burócrata* and *Memorias del subdesarrollo* as "experimental" films. Based on what has been previously considered, we could say that their "experimentalism" is marked by an eclectic will, a *collage* (this *collage* is also seen a bit, as satire, in *Memorias...*). However, as Zavarzaeh would say, we might fall into an "aestheticism" or a formalism that distracts us from the "whys" of the artwork itself.

Another irony is noted when one of the characters asks, "Where will his proletarian soul dwell?" with a lack of Marxist orthodoxy that borders on the ironic and satirical. This apparent lack of orthodoxy is repeated in the portrayal of the priest, shouting "wait, I'm going to confess him," while the people in the *confusion* understand that the protagonist wants to commit suicide. If there is no solace beyond, the pain of the proletarian, the martyrdom of the citizen in the bowels of bureaucracy becomes a double absurdity. On the other hand, the psychologist's function of defining his problem as an "Oedipus complex" accentuates the idea of "empty discourse," repeated, which we had already seen in the repeated busts of José Martí, in the cemetery's verbosity, and in the lawyer's explanation (an idea repeated in *Memorias del*

---

[20] We could understand that the nephew's dreams might owe something to surrealist cinema, except that they are clearly identified as "dreams" and not as waking states.

subdesarrollo in the panel of "intellectuals" from around the world)21. The psychologist's own "tics" confirm the parody and the absurdity, the disconnection between discourse and action (as will be seen when the bureaucrats organize a symbolic march against bureaucracy). The other connotation refers to Soviet psychiatric practices: the system, like any dominant ideology, only recognizes "decentered" (alienated) individuals.

We could close these notes on *La muerte de un burócrata* with the following idea from Zavarzaeh taken from Mannheim: "Ideology, according to Mannheim, protects its own 'truth' by constructing a coherent 'other'" (59).

Bibliography

Chanan, Michael. *Cuban Cinema*. Minneapolis: University of Minnesota Press, 2003.

Jaskari, Minna. "Tomás Gutiérrez Alea and the Post-Revolutionary Cuba." www.helsinki.fi/ hum/ ibero/ xaman/ articulos/ 9711/ 9711_mj.html

Zavarzaeh, Mas'ud. Seeing Films Politically. Nueva York: State University of New York. Press. 1991.

---

21 It has often been said that a writer writes and rewrites the same book. We could say that Gutiérrez Alea, like every artist with a creed, repeated other themes, such as that of bureaucracy using humor in Guantanamera. Among them, Chanan notably cites him through an anecdote involving Fidel Castro himself.

LUCÍA

García Espinosa and Tomas Gutiérrez Alea

Not by an Aristotelian principle, we always expect from any artistic proposal a unity that confers meaning to each part in relation to the whole, even when the proposal consists of a deliberate heterodoxy or a deliberate disconnection between the parts. In Lucía, we find none of this, but rather the opposite. The tripartite division not only recalls Greek unity but also Christian unity—and Catholic unity, above all. But in Lucía, unity is not just an aesthetic exercise but, above all, part of the narrative and the ideological discourse (understanding "ideological" here in a broad sense). Two of these "transcendent" unities stand out in its reading: Cuba —its history— and the three protagonists who, not by chance, share the same name, Lucía (star, light, dawn, etc.).

A first reading might tell us that Lucía is about the personal stories of three women. Alternatively, we could understand them—especially from a strictly feminist perspective, that is, in some cases, ideological—as the stories of the suffering of one gender subordinated to the other, the masculine, etc.

But I believe we could integrate these perspectives into a third one that, moreover, includes other readings in a coherent way: *Lucía* is the narrative of a "process" of historical consciousness-raising seen through three women. Each one represents a greater state of maturity. However, these three women, who are one in the metaphor that interests us, are, at the same time, Cuba or, in another way, Cuban society in its process of maturation. Now, in every process of maturation, it is assumed—whether in error or in correctness—that it is also a process of knowledge through experience and, consequently, of consciousness-raising. The ideological factor—now in its restricted, partisan sense—becomes evident and almost "ruins" the result when we notice that this peak moment of consciousness begins—since, fortunately, it does not culminate—in the Cuban Revolution. (22)

Within the unity we noted earlier, we can observe that each of the three parts could survive—artistically, as a narrative—independently. Three units that, in their chronological order, acquire a higher unity, which implies a structuralist reading.

Let's look at each part.

Perhaps it is the first of the three stories that best embodies these principles of unity. It even incorporates a relatively closed ending that gives coherence and meaning to the entire preceding narrative, which also aligns with one of the canonical principles of Western cinema and literature of the last two centuries.

---

22 We can see directly in Lucía III the portraits of José Martí and Fidel Castro, as the backdrop to a militarist-style moralizing discourse delivered by two of its protagonists.

In the Lucía of 1895, contrasts dominate a clear discourse: from a social class perspective—a central point in Marxist discourse—we see a group of women from the upper class, or at least "well-off," and another group of "untouchables"—in a Hindu sense—dramatically represented by Fernandina, the mad beggar (the "pelandruja"). Later, we will see how this judgment is paradoxically reversed. The "madwoman" is not the one who has lost reason or consciousness, but quite the opposite: she is the marginalized figure who possesses social consciousness—derived from a traumatic individual experience. The cry of "Wake up, Cubans!" is highly explicit in this regard. On the other hand, the woman from the upper class, the one "within the walls," remains in a state of ignorance until the end. ([23]) This state enables the final betrayal that becomes the key: the lack of *social consciousness* is the result of the death of her own brother—and, by extension, of all Cubans. The reasonable precept of "we win the war if we talk less and do more" becomes contradictory here, as it is not enough to

---

[23] We can note some similarities between these scenes of cloistered women and the drama of Federico García Lorca's *The House of Bernarda Alba*. In *Lucía*, Bernarda is not within walls, but outside. The same gesture of spying on what happens outside—in society—through half-open windows indicates this submission and unconsciousness, as well as repression. Here, Bernarda has sublimated into the "super-ego" (in its psychoanalytic sense) to become the political-social power, the Empire. Recall that in Lorca's drama, this authority expressed political-social power but in an inverse sense: the abstraction was embodied in a woman inside the house.

"do" without consciousness, without that consciousness that could be represented by "talking more." The "doing" of Lucía I is, in reality, an "undoing." When she "rebels," her rebellion has tragic consequences for herself; it is a rebellion with a meaning contrary to itself. *Lucía I*, the spinster, is trapped in matters of the heart, in the laws of a society that strictly determines female roles, the same laws that R... will use to play his political game and win. Lucía I finally gains the consciousness that the beggar had, but it is too late. [24] Her act is simply a criminal act, one of (just) vengeance. However, in terms of social change, it is almost insignificant. It could even serve to maintain the *status quo* [25] with greater aggressiveness. It is not a political crime— like those of Lucía II will be—but a crime of passion, an individual one.

In Lucía II, the class and gender division of Lucía I is confirmed: women are outside of history. Their stories are individual (the "matters of the heart") and tend toward the

---

[24] The Fernandina warns Lucía: "Don't go with him." This is the key phrase that will reveal the rest of the plot. But Lucía is not aware of this plot and *chooses* not to listen, as her reality is constructed from other codes where the problem of the individual obscures the transcendent issues of her own action. Another beggar, at the end, will be the one who indicates where Rafael is ("in the square"), revealing and confirming that the "consciousness" of the *plot* lies not in the protagonists so much as in their marginalized class.

[25] Earlier, one of the old women inside the walls had declared, "One must know how to endure trials with resignation."

frivolous [26]. The world of men, on the other hand, is the world of history. Their lovers do not reveal a concern for the emotional but, precisely, the opposite: it is a lack of concern, the restorative and functional rest of the subject who makes history. However, in Lucía II, the same change occurs that we can see between Lucía I and Lucía II: from the individual to the social, from unconsciousness to consciousness, etc.

Lucía II is represented by her own mother at the beginning: "You are a sweet, pleasant, innocent woman." This, along with the image of youth and fragility of Lucía II, completes the construction of the feminine (the "eternal feminine"). And the corresponding symptom: "I spend my life in silence," which corresponds to the advice given to women in Lucía I. Like Lucía I, Lucía II—in her first stage—says: "That day I was happy because Aldo confessed he loved me" [27].

We could say that Gutiérrez Alea, like all great artists, focuses the lens on an individual drama to show a process—or a problem—that transcends the individual themselves. In this case, we can see that the individual is the intersection of the forces of history, as a passive object (Lucía I) and

---

[26] "Your father has a mistress. And they say she's ugly." The daughter comments: "She only talks about her friends, about games of canasta," etc.

[27] Lucía I's confession of "I'm happy" is made to Felipe, in stark contrast to the social drama that was unfolding.

as an active subject of their (part of) destiny (Lucía II and Lucía III).

The failure of the revolution against Machado underscores the idea of "incomplete social consciousness" while, not innocently, it does not prepare for a higher stage: the Revolution. Lucía III, on the other hand, while representing this higher stage, simultaneously indicates that the task is not finished but, on the contrary, continues. Now the enemy is no longer political power but the very lack of consciousness in the rest of the population that maintains the codes (machista, to take one) of the old order. Nor is the idea that the "defense of women's rights" is based on the Revolution presented innocently, as if these rights and gender changes were not a more universal phenomenon throughout the history of the last hundred years. The black couple in Lucía III, despite being older than the male protagonist, is presented from a superior position that should serve as a lesson in the new ethical virtues of the times created by the new regime. The tone of this last part is openly humorous and subtly propagandistic. Which we can understand as a critique in itself if we discard an unsuspected conformism on the part of Gutiérrez Alea.

Lucía II also begins like the previous ones, identifying the feminine with love, boyfriends, and clothes: with the intimate space.

These three stories are a narrative about the maturation of a society but, paradoxically, told through three central protagonists, three individuals, three specific women. The

generic Lucía matures, acquires greater social consciousness, while simultaneously "descending" in class: from the
upper, aristocratic class (1895), to the upper-middle and
then lower-middle, bourgeois class (1932), until the last,
who belongs to the peasant class, in addition to being a
"guajira" (196...)[28]. The conflict is expressed not only
through artistic choice but also—and we assume intention-
ally—through the ideology of the filmmakers. That is, in
the first Lucía, the individual appears as central, the only
apparent subject of existence, independent of social problems but ultimately trapped by them. The social problem
transcends the individual, but the individual does not become aware of it—a Marxist trait—until it is too late because they have served as an instrument of the prevailing
social system. In the other two Lucías, we can see that the
narrative *from* the individual begins to connect with the social until it almost merges with it. It is the moment of *social
consciousness*, the pinnacle state for Lucía's ideology.

The women of Lucía I are not protagonists of history,
of their history; they are simply instruments. We will see

---

[28] Perhaps the paradoxical aspect is that this new morality (loftier), this
new state of consciousness, is not expressed so much *from* the individual,
but *from* the State. And the most superficial paradox is realized when
"consciousness" is injected by two orators among a passive audience, using an absolutely militaristic discourse. It is not, precisely, in the army
where soldiers gain greater consciousness: a soldier is not virtuous because of his questioning, his individuality, his freedom of thought, but
quite the opposite: because of his unrestricted and unreflective obedience.

that in Lucía II and the last Lucía, this process will intensify: from the passivity of the object to the protagonism of the subject. In this sense, Lucía II is, in itself, the pivot, the turning point between Lucía I and Lucía III. Lucía II begins with traits of its predecessor and ends by anticipating the traits of its successor.

Symbolic elements

Of course, symbolic elements could not be absent. Quickly (because perhaps they are not central to the narrative "logic") we can note some historical associations. For example, the recurrence of the figure of the staked prisoner has strong Christian connotations, in the crucifixion, while also recalling the sacrifice of Túpac Amaru—which also refers us to the martyrdom of the former. However, both the reference to Túpac Amaru and that of the prisoners hanging in a row under an arch are related to the iconography that, after Bartolomé de las Casas, the nascent British Empire created with a clear political objective: the black legend of Spain, the cruelty dramatized through images that, unlike Guamán Poma Ayala, do not come from witnesses but from "interpreters." It is also symbolic that Fernandina (the mad-conscious beggar) was the daughter of an Arab who arrived fleeing, which takes us back to the years of the Reconquista and, even further, to the years of the "purification" that Spain attempted in the subsequent centuries. Also, the fact that Fernandina is a nun cannot be a coincidence. She could have been a prostitute or any other woman in Cuban society. However, the rape of a nun not only increases the drama—which further justifies the victim's madness—but also symbolically relates to the violation of the principles that justified the domination of the Spanish Empire in America: evangelization.

The hysterical laughter of the upper-class women can be interpreted as another sign of that (social) unconsciousness[29]. Her task is alienating, her social role as well. The result is not only frivolity but also the swan song before death, represented in *Lucía II* by alcohol. The rape of Fernandina aligns with this perspective: the drama of the woman with a new consciousness is narrated with frivolity and joy: "the party began right there," says one of them. The solution to the drama: a mechanical and anesthetic "pray for us."

The change of Lucía's name by Rafael can be symbolic: he turns her into "Gardenia," a flower, a stereotype of the feminine, of passivity, fragility, and the tropical. ([30]) In the dialogue between Lucía I and Rafael, it is the man who asks the questions, while the woman apologizes for having tried. Her posture must be one of shyness and passivity. Of slight resistance. When Rafael asks her if she wants to get

---

[29] A false unconsciousness is represented by Rafael's discourse: "I'm not interested in politics. I'm not on the side of either the Cubans or the Spaniards."
[30] In *Memories of Underdevelopment*, Sergio will say: "In the tropics, everything ripens and decays easily; nothing persists."

married, a minimal internal questioning arises in her doubt. Later, the "overacting" in the ruins suggests a hidden functionality in the acts that are taking place.

But if at any moment there were doubts on the part of Lucía I, the social formula will be stronger, and in the end, erotic passion, the final trait of unconsciousness. Perhaps it is unnecessary to note that the game of "blind man's buff" is deeply symbolic and consonant with the previous observations. It is no coincidence that Lucía must play this role in the game and in the rest of the plot. In clear contrast, this game of "blind man's buff" becomes dramatic with the one who has consciousness but is defined as "crazy" and, moreover, belongs to a class of untouchables (or unmentionables). Here, the children's game turns into a new series of aggressions and violations: the social problem is personalized by stigmatizing it in an individual, who simply serves the function of pus in an infection.

In Lucía II we will find these elements in "the house in the keys," in the allusions to tennis—a symbol of social class and distant from popular Cuban practices.

THE CRIME OF FATHER AMARO

Carlos Carrera, Alfredo and Daniel Ripstein, 2002.

The Ethical Triumph of Defeat

Father Amaro

The Crime of Father Amaro begins with a scene that will be powerfully significant for the reinterpretation of the events that will later unfold, in a cascade, like a game of dominoes: before the young priest sets foot in the town, before he steps onto the ground, the bus that was taking him to his destination is assaulted. Father Amaro suffers no significant loss. The one who loses, the one who is beaten, as always, is a representative of the people. This representative, before the assault, had commented to the priest about his intentions:

Old passenger: —I'm going to open a store with a grandson. If the store doesn't work out, then I'll leave for the other side. I have a daughter there.

With these few words, the old man painted a concise picture of the current moment of a common Mexican: his daughter has gone to the United States and has left her son with him to take care of while she sorts out her economic situation. The old man still tries new possibilities —with the younger generation—, though he is skeptical about the success of his last effort.

But he is assaulted and the little money he has is taken from him. The perfect moment to profile the protagonist: before getting off the bus, the young priest gives money to the poor old man.

Here we have the religious man. Only we don't yet know if the young priest is a good person or if he is constructing an image of himself. That is, he did what a good man —and, above all, a good priest— should do: he was compassionate, generous, sensitive to the pain of others. Later, he will even "confess" to Father Benito his intentions: "I only want to serve God." Which, in an indirect way, Father Benito, with a less clean, wrinkled conscience, warns that "a barking priest doesn't bite"[31].

However, by the end of the film we can make a different reading: then, the young priest paid his dues, passed the test, acted out of duty, not out of consideration for the *other*, but *for himself*.

The same reading can be made of the incident where Amalia's fiancé hits him in the street. Father Amaro does not react. When taken to declare before the police, the priest drops the charges in front of Ruben himself, which enrages him even more, leading him to attempt to attack the priest again.

---

[31] Later, after showing him where he will live, Father Benito says: "Perhaps you'll stay for a short time, if you manage to please me and the bishop." That is, if he is obedient —not to God but to the religious authorities— his career to Rome will be meteoric.

76

Father Amaro's attitude aims to be Christian: in the face of aggression, he turns the other cheek; in the face of the possibility of condemnation, he forgives.

However, these attitudes, while they manage to win the sympathy of the viewer, will ultimately reveal themselves as false —even arrogant— in their decisive moment. Father Amaro is less direct and frank than the young journalist. He is the true hypocrite. He is playing a role assigned by Catholic tradition. He is an actor32 who must convince the people and, above all, the bishop, since his career depends on the latter.

When Amalia tells him she is pregnant, Father Amaro has no qualms about trying to get rid of his problem-child. He suggests having the baby in another town and giving it up for adoption.33 He even hits her. He dismisses the driver without a hint of pity for his indiscretion, leaving the man, who must carry the invalid like a piece of furniture on a donkey-drawn cart, out on the street. After this expulsion, the lovers will continue to have sex in the same place, confirming not only their indifference to the pain of others but also their selfishness.

---

32 The great actor is Lucifer. The actors, the simulators, are his disciples. The great simulation is to represent the Demiurge as God, as the Gnostics of the early centuries of Christianity claimed before the Council of Nicaea (325 AD) condemned them and later official Christianity pursued them until their extinction. This also aligns with the idea of the church driver: "It seems to me the devil came to this town years ago."

33 "I cannot risk my apostleship," he says.

As if that weren't enough, Father Amaro will ultimately hand over his "beloved" to her former boyfriend, who will have to take responsibility for her child, thus saving him from the shame and frustration of his brilliant career.34

However, *Father Amaro* knows how to play only one role, the one taught to him in the seminary, the role of the good Christian. But when he faces the contaminated reality of the town, the false relationships that prevail among his superiors and the environment that surrounds him, he fails. He becomes a terrible actor. He lies and doesn't know how. He is unconvincing.

The height of this unconvincingness is reached when he tries to justify his encounters with the girl. *"Amalia, a very pious girl* —he says to everyone he meets—. *She wants to be a nun. I want to prepare her* [but in secret]"

When the truth calls, Father Amaro does not respond. Finally, he will take advantage of the favorable prejudice the townspeople have of him, after Amalia's death, blaming the young journalist for her death.35 A lie that the young priest firmly upholds with his silence.

---

[34] Father Amaro prays: "Do not let me sink."

Social Groups

In *The Crime of Father Amaro* we can identify very defined social groups that not only correspond to economic groups but also to more or less defined ethical groups.

The first major group —not because of its size but because of its importance in the film— is the group of religious figures. It's obvious. But within this group, there are, in turn, antagonistic groups: first, there is the "officialist group," made up of Father Benito, the bishop, and Father Amaro himself. On the other hand, there is the "heretical group," represented by Father Natalio. He, Father Natalio, is a probable militant of Liberation Theology and a probable guerrilla fighter. What is certain, at least from the film's discourse, is that Father Natalio's group represents everything that the officialist Catholic group lacks: scruples, ethical principles, selflessness, solidarity with the oppressed and persecuted, authenticity in their discourse, correspondence between their preaching and their actions. For many moments, Father Amaro risks crossing the line that separates these groups from the officialists. But at every moment, his obedience to religious authorities triumphs, which is nothing more than obedience to his own personal ambitions. When he brings Father Natalio the news of excommunication36, he does so with the awareness that it is the most serious thing that can

---

[36] He doesn't even consider moving from the town for a second time, as the bishop had suggested, as a condition to avoid excommunication.

happen to a priest in his career, that is, in his life. With tears in his eyes, he says: "now you are outside the Church." Being "outside" the Church means "being nobody," losing all identity, all hope, all purpose in life. But Father Amaro does not only cry for the gravity of this fact but because, deep down, he overvalues Father Natalio: "Believe me, I admire you, Natalio," he says, before leaving him. Undoubtedly, he admires him: Natalio is capable of doing what he knows is most noble, but which he himself cannot do. His career is above his own ethical values, and he will never resolve this contradiction, at least not by eliminating the weakest factor, that is, the ethical factor, the scruples37.

On the other hand, we find the people, represented by the young Amalia, the church driver, and the rest of the characters who do something useful for others. This people —the Mexican people— never appear revealed; when they do appear, it is in a typical manner, like the construction workers of Father Benito who whistle at Amalia as she walks through the construction site—, part of the obligatory folklore of a machista and Latin American society.[38]

---

[37] When Amalia proposes that he renounce his vows to marry her, he refuses, claiming that "what's important" is his vocation. Though he quickly adds—, justifying himself—: *"Besides*, as a priest I can do much for the people."

[38] This town also appears at one point as part of the psychological structure of ecclesiastical domination when, after hearing an incoherent sermon from Father Amaro, they take to the streets in a fury to protest the newspaper and support Father Benito. Father Amaro does not incite this violence, but the "solidarity" of the "members" belonging to the base of

In ideological opposition to the group of religious figures, we find the atheists, the anticlericals represented by the journalists, the newspaper editor, and the chess players.

A necessary, though stereotyped group[39], is that of the drug traffickers, which, of course, will be related to all the groups that, in some way, hold power in Mexico: government, Church, commerce, etc. Unlike the Colombian case, where the supposed "subversive" groups are part of the contradictory dialectic of power, in The Crime of Father Amaro the "resistant" group of Father Natalio opposes it. Also for this reason —because "power" and "corruption" have become synonymous, if they were ever anything else— it is that the rebel priest represents the good that has not yet been commercialized.40

A third group is represented by a single character: the santera, in the name of the marginalized, the insane, the

---

the Church exacerbates and slips away from the mediocre preacher. Here we see Father Amaro again, the young priest, the "tender" priest filling a gap in an ecclesiastical ideology that moves on its own, that makes its lower members act, that uses them, transforms them, and molds them.
[39] Another minor group that is stereotyped is the politicians governing the town. I believe it's the mayor who says mockingly: "I govern for my town, not for my party."
[40] I believe everything regarding the groups of drug traffickers and Chato Aguilar could have been omitted, avoided with a more suggestive absence. The party, the guards dressed as cowboys, are implausible or poorly acted. The password made by Father Benito, drawing a cross in the air and uttering the keyword "shark," is more fitting for a weekend cop show binge than for a film that prides itself on being "Latin American."

unscrupulous like the authorities and the powerful, a for-tune-teller, matchmaker, and evil witch.

All these groups, including Father Natalio's group, are marked by simulation and lies. In the latter case and in the case of the santera, it is for reasons of survival; in the other cases, it will always be for personal ambitions never satisfied.

Everyone knows, for example, that celibacy is the Great Lie. But no one wants to admit it:

Amalia's Mother: [*Upon meeting Father Amaro*] —My daughter had already told me, very young and handsome.

Father Benito: —Priests are neither young nor hand-some. They are ministers of God.

At another moment, the Mayor's wife confesses and, be-fore handing Father Amaro an envelope with money, suppos-edly from drug trafficking, she says:

The Mayor's Wife: —Now that you know my sins, I want [to invite you to my house so that] you may know my virtues.

Ethical and Psychological Types

The encounter between the priest and the girl he falls for happens in a somewhat conventional way: some children are playing ball, and the ball —an innocent object— escapes and lands near him, who, after watching it approach, hands it to her. The orange ball is full of symbolism. It not only signifies a "physical dialogue," the first contact, but also a "giving," a "possession." As she receives the offering, she looks into his eyes. What in street language is called "love at first sight."

This clandestine relationship is born and spreads like fire. It cannot be hidden, and when the protagonists try to do so, they do it very poorly. From the beginning, the girl's boyfriend notices the fact. It won't be long before the old santera does the same, with greater eloquence. The looks are evident, and finally, the first kiss will be in the most public of public spaces, a village church. The same will happen with the place the priest finds to make love to the girl, the excuses he uses to hide the fact, etc.

From the beginning of *The Crime of Father Amaro*, the father of her boyfriend gives a clue to Amelia's personality: the girl has her head full of "prayers," thanks to the "idiots41" of the priests.

But this head full of "prayers" will express in its own way the sensuality that cannot be contained at that age:

Amalia: [*At Father Benito's construction site*] "I'm not in love with my boyfriend. [...] I am in love with God."

With the exception of Father Natalio, all the other characters share the same lack: scruples. The santera is a marginal character, but she has not reached her poverty due to ethical, religious, or philosophical reasons, which is quickly demonstrated when the collection is taken in the church: the old woman leaves a few coins and, with the same hand, picks up a bill. The santera is corrupt and uses her skills to take advantage of the situation for her own benefit. She will do the

---

41 Not only because of this insulting term, but because of his references to Franco, we deduce that he is a Spanish immigrant.

same with the hosts and with young Amalia, when she arranges a clandestine hospital to perform the abortion. Not much different is what the ecclesiastical authorities do —including Father Amaro, of course—, the journalists, and the drug traffickers.

Part of the lie is justifying the contradictions between desire and duty, between dogma and practice; part of the lie consists in leaping over the laws of the Church to avoid stepping on them.

An example of this briefly illustrates the previous observation:

Father Amaro: "Tell me your sins."

Amalia: "I like being sensual. I touch myself when I bathe and the water runs over my body. Is it a sin?"

Father Amaro: "No, it is not a sin. The body and the soul are the same essence."

Of course, it would not be the same essence if it were the body and soul of an old woman and not the woman that Father Amaro desired.

And immediately Amalia adds:

Amalia: "I think it is Jesus who touches me. Is that a sin?"

Father Amaro: "Yes, it is a sin."

The same Father Amaro will be the one who, before making love to her, compares her to the Virgin Mary and concludes that she is more beautiful.

Father Benito will also assert, emphatically, that the idea of abolishing celibacy is "nonsense."

84

Even clearer, the idea previously mentioned is evident in the following dialogue:

Father Benito: "Money for good works should not be questioned."

Father Amaro: "It's laundered money."

Father Benito: "The true laundering is before God."

The same rhetorical position is that of the Bishop, with a rationality that was common in Martin Luther (also a Christian, yes, but an enemy):

Bishop: "Where sin abounds, the grace of God will abound even more. For God, everything has a remedy."

It will be because of the Bishop —that is, because of the authority, the system— that Father Amaro will begin to practice the game of lies, extortion, and unscrupulous strategy to achieve personal results. It is precisely when the new priest goes to speak with the newspaper editor who published an article denouncing the Church's ties to the guerrillas, a link that appears as probable, not proven, but, in any case, is not presented as a perverse link but, on the contrary, as a link with the victims of the mountains, the victims of drug trafficking and the government.

Father Amaro: [*To the newspaper editor*] —Does the truth depend on the readers or the ads? I say this because the bishop can end the advertising...

A brief dialogue between Father Benito and his lover confirms the contradiction not only between discourse and actions, but also between discourse and thought:

Father Benito: "I turned you into the priest's whore."

Benito's Woman: "You once told me that the only hell is loneliness."

Father Benito: "Did I say that? I wish I understood it that way."

Symbolism

It is unnecessary to mention that *The Crime of Father Amaro* will be full of sensuality, until the attraction between the young priest and the girl is consummated. He is driven by desire; she is driven by love. This position in the drama is also anachronistic, but let us not forget that the film is based on a novel written at the end of the 19th century. Now, Carlos Carrera must resolve, using images, this sensuality. Resources of the liturgy will not be lacking. If he gave the host to a cat, why wouldn't he use it to create a sensual image on the altar itself? I refer to the moment when Father Amaro places the host in young Amalia's mouth. The identification of Jesus with the Passion is double, and it has probably always been so. Images of Jesus will also appear when Father Amaro and Amalia begin their carnal relationship.

The place where the young "sinners" will make love repeatedly is preceded by a long wall full of stains. The symbolism is too direct.

It is not as direct but is still striking and significant, the role played by the paralyzed woman. She —like all the women in the town— falls in love with Father Amaro. And, as one of the most impactful scenes that *The Crime of Father

Amaro* could produce, the paralyzed woman suffers from the sex her beloved has with another young woman —with a beautiful young woman. Thus, the cries of pleasure from the act are replaced by the cries of deep despair from the paralyzed woman. She is the purest embodiment of physical and moral pain.

On the other hand, we have the formal opponents. I refer to the newspaper editor and the people around him, all of them anticlerical. This is not only "suggested" by the repeated scenes showing them playing chess, but they are also *the bearers of the written word that does not obey God*. The newspaper also generates awareness and opinion among the people, but not in the name of God and, as will be seen in the film, in an openly anticlerical manner —which results in the most important clash between these two groups.

However, the true opponent is within the structure and within the tradition of the Church, emerging from it and expelled as a heretic. Father Natalio, the rebel priest, is the only one in his church who wears a beard. The beard not only represents the dissenter but also brings him closer to the image of the primitive Christian —the original. His commitment to the oppressed is real, not just in words. He preaches in the mountains, in a hostile environment; his church is a precarious construction that they build with their own hands —a task in which Father Amaro participates only symbolically, during one of his visits to the "real world."

On a lesser note, let us observe that Amaro and Amalia are similar. We should not analyze this coincidence as a de facto fact, as hermeneutics on an ancient religious text, or as a mysterious and revealing product of the unconscious. It barely serves to uncover a conscious game by the authors of *The Crime of Father Amaro*.

It is important, in this analytical summary of the film's symbols, to highlight the physical appearance of the protagonist. Gael García Bernal is what one might call a handsome young man. His masculinity is not strongly accentuated —by Western standards—. There is an almost feminine profile, that is, delicate, innocent, angelic, and —one must assume— sensual. The character also supports this profile with his performance: from the beginning, Father Amaro presents himself as a kind and innocent young man, with noble values, willing to help others, the poor, the ugly. He is a kind of angel who charms all the women in the town. From the old women to the paralyzed woman who clings to his arm with the strength she lacks. One does not expect from him the revelation that, after the extortion of the newspaper editor, will begin to unfold moment by moment. Even so, the trust in his physical appearance makes one hope for a vindication of his worth in a final confession that will never come. Instead, the irremediable cowardice, selfishness, or —worse— the cold and dark consciousness of the antichrist will prevail.

Among the symbolisms, we can note an important group of contrasts:

Contrasts, parody, and irony

When Father Amaro enters what will be his church, the first thing he hears is a song from the old healer: it is cartoon-ish, aggressively out of tune, almost on the verge of parody and blasphemy42. As if that were not enough, this same woman will use the hosts as food for her cats, with the added offense of saying it explicitly: "take your medicine, it's the body of Christ." Later, we will find the same symbol "de-sacralized" almost to the point of blasphemy, represented by a group of children eating hosts with ketchup.43 In another later scene, this same atmosphere will be shown as a surrealist combination of cats and dolls. And, almost at the end, when Father Amaro goes to seek the healer to find a doctor who will abort his child, the old woman tells him: "This is my pri-vate church," and then shows him the saints she has col-lected.

An ethical-theological contrast or contradiction occurs when Father Amaro, knowing of Amalia's pregnancy, prays to the Virgin asking for a miracle. That miracle comes: Ama-lia agrees to have the abortion.44

---

42 He sings: "The angels sing and praise God."

43 An ethical issue in production arises here when children—, minors—, are used to portray a scene with such strong religious and symbolic weight. We cannot know what moral rejection they might have in ten or fifteen years.

44 Father Amaro claims that Amalia is free to have the abortion of her own volition. This has a double effect: 1) The priest does not take respon-sibility for the decision to abort his own child; 2) he doesn't impose a dic-tatorial decision on a woman, though he pressures her to make a decision favorable to his desire: the abortion. There will be a moment of sincerity

There is also a contrast that is, at the same time, a new simulation: the bells that originally rang in the bell tower have been replaced by a recording played through loudspeakers.[45] A similar contrast happens when Father Benito takes off in the drug trafficker's plane to be treated in a distant hospital. The flight is accompanied by a religious, almost Gregorian, choir.

Contrast or discordance with clothing: when Amalia goes to take "classes to become a nun," she appears as the young virgin among dirty walls, among unpainted doors —which we already saw as an allegory—. But also, Amalia's nun uniform is completely contradictory: a miniskirt.

A final contrast —part of Father Amaro's performance, part of the lie of the ecclesiastical discourse— is confirmed by Father Amaro himself when he officiates the mass before Amalia's body: he calls her "Sister Amalia."

The paralyzed woman also represents a cruel contrast with the young couple making love in the next room: the voluptuousness of sex and the immobility of the sick woman; the cries of pleasure and the almost silent moans of the paralyzed woman.

---

when, awaiting the outcome of the abortion, he tells the grandfather-passenger he meets at the clandestine hospital: "[I didn't come to help any girl] I came to be helped myself."

[45] This is not an invention of the film. It exists in many churches, and it's not explained why the old bells are problematic but rather the physical discomfort of moving those giant, noble bronze masses.

Another contrast, this time ethical, occurs in the same scene. Father Amaro goes in search of someone to kill a fetus, saying: "I'm looking for a doctor to bring children into the world"

But, since Father Amaro is never credible, he has never learned to lie despite having done so repeatedly since arriving in the town, and, moreover, because he is seeking to be discovered, hoping that the other will do what he cannot do —tell the truth—, and because the healer is very perceptive, she immediately notices and replies:

Healer: —"What you want is an abortion, Father."

Father Amaro gives her money, and she responds:

Healer: —"May God bless you, Father."

This dialectic of ethical-symbolic contrasts will also be confirmed when Father Benito baptizes the drug trafficker's daughter. The ceremony is brief and presented as a mandatory formality done with the utmost diligence before the party, like the hurried prayer of a hungry man precedes the annihilation of a banquet. The Christian ceremony is only the justification and appearance of the party dedicated to the true god: Bacchus.

A final and tragic contrast is made by the choir singing at Amalia's funeral mass:

> *Jesus called you*
> *To be with Him*
> *He will wait for you*
> *With open arms*

Father, I come to You.

Humor

The Crime of Father Amaro is both a drama and a comedy at the same time. As is the norm, the comedic events come well before the drama, which, invariably, must come at the end. This order is inverted in dominant American films, but not in a Latin American genre that does not aim to entertain —relax, that is the function of laughter after tension— but, on the contrary, aims to be more moving and, if possible, critical.

So in the first half, we will find expressions like:

Amalia: "Don't you believe in God?"

Boyfriend: "Maybe. But I don't like priests."

Amalia: "Are you a communist?"

Which, by the way, serves as an ironic critique of the naive popular perspective, dominated by the discourse of the dominant ideology.

Or when, after making love with the priest, Amalia teaches the Ten Commandments and changes the meaning of the sixth: "Thou shalt not fornicate means you won't eat meat during Lent."

The Crime of Father Amaro is an openly anticlerical film, deliberately provocative. Its strategies are sometimes humor and irony, and above all, the explicit exposure of the double standards of the representatives of the Catholic Church. By highlighting these serious contradictions, it also exposes the illegitimacy of power, not only religious but also political and economic. Of course, this film does not deal with new topics, nor even in a novel way —The bird sings until it dies resembles it. The book it is based on is from the 19th century.

However, the timing is appropriate. It is necessary *to remind* the forgetful of the hidden tradition: the moral and discursive corruption of priests, their pedophilia, their false celibacy, their false love, their false sacrifice for the sake of others. Of course, it also runs the risk of provoking its own witch hunt...

A reading through Mas'ud Zavarzaeh

For Zavarzaeh, the relationship between the center and the margin is one of opposition —conflictual— between exclusion and inclusion. Its crisis is one of the symptoms of Postmodernity46.

However, what exactly does "crisis" in the traditional relationship between the center and the margin mean? Undoubtedly, this has not changed since the Neolithic: there is a center from which a predominant discourse is emitted, which is, at the same time, exclusionary. Those who are harmed by this discourse or who resist it must, necessarily,

---

46 *"[The] relation between the center and the margin [...] is itself a symptom of the crisis of Postmodernity and uncertainty about the norms that might 'justify' and 'explain' the acts one undertakes."* Mas'ud Zavarzaeh, Seeing Films Politically, pg. 169. State University of New York Press, Albany, 1991.

position themselves on the margin. The crisis of this dialectical relationship means, above all, an awareness and an ethical questioning of this relationship, long before a structural —spatial— change of the traditional center.

Now, how does the center subjugate, and how does the margin defend itself, how does the margin react, and how does the center reorganize?

It is important to note that the center is the main producer of "legitimations," that is, the main author of the predominant ethical discourse. But this discourse needs an enemy: the margin. Personally, I believe that one of the strengths of the center in relation to the *res intermedia*[47] lies in maintaining a clear ethical-symbolic relationship with the margin. That is, the center needs the margin. Without danger and threat, there could be no effective ideological domination. It is for this reason that the center must combat the ethical-contestatory emergence of the margin, but never completely suppress it. If a margin did not exist —dialectically made impossible— the center would invent it.

A second form of "ideological manipulation" practiced by the center, apart from antagonism, is "absorption." What we could also call "integration of exclusion" or "nullification of dissent."[48]

---

[47] With this term of questionable understanding, I refer to the social body situated between the center and the margin, which surely constitutes the social majority.
[48] [Hollywood films] *attempt to recuperate the radical margin as a 're-formist' discourse. The margin and its discourses, in a gesture of open-*

What remains unclear is whether the center is plural or not. We know that the margin is, but the answer is not so clear when we interrogate the center. Two possibilities arise: a) the center is unique, by ideological nature and hierarchical organization; or b) the center is a "coherent" plurality, that is, capable of integrating the different levels and categories of domination discourses: racial, class, economic, gender, etc. —a woman of the dominant class would, in some way and at the same time, be marginal due to her sex.

From this perspective, *The Crime of Father Amaro* constructs a discourse that, likely originating in the center, consciously positions itself on the margin. We know that a fundamental part of the dominant ideology, the "central" ideology, consists of associating the margin with ethical disqualifiers, such as those of social, sexual, or productive order. That is, the margin is unproductive, disorderly, dangerous to order and security, sexually deviant or unnatural, immature, etc.

In Hollywood films, the margin ultimately integrates into the center —the hippie, the bohemian, the dissenter, the "libertine" woman, etc. But not only as a way to "reform" some dysfunctional elements of the center —which it must help to regain its own centrality in times of "deviation"—, but by recognizing itself as incapable of serious changes and

---

mindedness, are seen as having a 'positive' effect on the center." Op. Cit. p. 170. "[in *Desperately Seeking Susan*] margin that can form a moral coalition with the center" Op. cit. pg. 178.

as a characteristic of psychological, ideological, productive, and moral immaturity.

On the contrary, in *The Crime of Father Amaro* the center ultimately triumphs in the plot, which signifies a necessary ethical defeat in the meta-plot, that is, in the probable readings of the viewer. The center is morally corrupt.

There is also a paradox that, although it may surprise, is by no means a property of postmodernity but rather of the origins of Christianity: the center represents strength and social power, domination, *while simultaneously embodying ethical marginality.* From this perspective, this discourse is marginal. Only the power of the dominant can impose censorship of expression; but the censor is, historically, the one who has lost the battle for ethical legitimacy, because their discourse is insufficient.

Father Natalio represents the typical marginalized figure: he is in political and ecclesiastical clandestinity. He is also marginalized by political and civil power, represented by the town's newspaper. However, he is the only "ethical hero" who stands out in the discourse of *The Crime of Father Amaro*. His defeat, the excommunication —the definitive separation from corruption and power— like that of Jesus, is the only effective form of moral triumph.

THE SON OF THE BRIDE

Juan José Campanella, 2001

Introduction

In *The Son of the Bride* there is an initial satire of the contemporary world, represented fundamentally in the figure of Rafael (Ricardo Darín) and his already classic relationship with his cell phone.

As could not be otherwise, society filters into the family and personal stories, but in this case it does so consciously: the Argentine economic crisis, the corruption of public relations, etc.

However, there persists —and it is the reason for that very conflict— the tradition of friendship and "family," accentuated in the Río de la Plata (specifically Buenos Aires) by the Italian tradition. The characters belong to a typical family of Italian immigrants.

But the crisis (the crossroads) is not only economic but also represents a change in personal relationships. The new ways of life filter through the old ones to produce a negative change, most of the time. In *The Son of the Bride* this change is represented by the stressful world of business that demands the son to live for and by his work, in contrast to the idyllic world of his father who, together with his mother, was able to start the restaurant and develop it in a romantic, rather than purely materialistic, way. Even so, the madness of the career is not enough. It barely allows him to avoid falling into the economic crisis and foreign competition but at a very high cost: Rafael's health and the deterioration of his affective relationships. These are not only represented in his inability to communicate with his partners and his daughter —who feels ignored—, but also in his relationship with his mother.

However, here another dimension of *The Son of the Bride* emerges, which transcends the protagonist's present: the emotional commerce with his mother, through affective signs, has been equally unsatisfactory and, when it seemed to have been resolved by a workaholic pursuit of success, it reveals itself as immutable, like a pending debt that, due to his mother's illness, seems impossible to pay.

I believe it is also worth noting the constant contrasts and *inversions* that occur in *The Son of the Bride*. There are notable inversions of thematic focuses, of discursive planes —the filming and the "secondary" scenes—, the inversion of religious meaning —the religious ritual in the church—, the inversion of the path initiated by the father is reversed by him, the apparent "betrayal" of the friend that serves to draw attention to his love relationship, his —classic—return to the past in rescue of the present, all of which expresses an *inversion in the meaning* of life: what is the purpose of our actions? Success or affection? To listen or to be heard? Etc.

Development

The Son of the Bride begins with a scene that we know —by its narrative and photographic technique, by its costumes, by intuition— belongs to the childhood of one of the protagonists. Children playing with an old ball, in a marginal, destroyed setting, almost a cemetery, wearing jerseys of Buenos Aires football clubs, Boca and River, develop a "small" childish power conflict. It is the moment when the *Fox* (Rafael Belverdere, in his childhood) appears with a slingshot to bring justice. It might be intentional that the Fox wears the Boca Juniors jersey —representing the popular, to the extreme— and is pursued by his classic sporting and neighborhood rival, River Plate, the "millionaires." This, like many other scenes in the film, is classic: the righteous child will become something else, but he will never forget his ideal past and will make sure to translate and repeat it as a legitimization of his future actions. When he becomes a gastronomic entrepreneur, he will remind his father —or, rather, will put in his father's mouth— that he taught him to fight for "ideals." To which his father (Héctor Alterio) will deny it using parody and humor.

After the nostalgic images of childhood —a trademark of the Río de la Plata, of the philosophy of tango, the protective affection of "the grandma"— the present bursts in with all its madness —also archetypal—: the same owner of the blue eyes eats hurriedly, while working, ordering, and talking on his cell phone at all times and in any place.

Emphasizing this image of postmodern alienation, the cell phone is erased from the image by using the microphone and earpiece (which allows talking without stopping "working"), which reinforces a pathetic image: the new worker, the entrepreneur talks to himself, he is as alienated as his mother. Or more —as will be suggested in many parts of the film.

Inversions

When some speculators offer Rafael to sell the restaurant, they try to persuade him by saying it is a time of crisis. To which Rafael responds:

Rafael: — When hasn't there been a crisis? There has always been a crisis. We live in a permanent crisis.

That is, the crisis —the exception— is the norm, the rule. The exceptional in a crazy world, which has lost the meaning of its action, is the rule.

When Rafael's mother repeatedly asks her granddaughter what her name is, and she responds: "Victoria," immediately her father, Rafael, explains that "the grandmother repeats things because she is sick," to which the daughter —marginal due to her age— responds, with a tired gesture: "I know; *you've told me hundreds of times*." The inversion consists, of course, in the conclusion: the alienated one, the one who does not understand and repeats, is Rafael.

When Rafael hits an employee because he is slow and inefficient, he does it in the name of "The champion of justice," humorously mimicking the "Z" of the childhood hero. However, his violent action is directed at a marginal individual, without power. It is a "Z" that is not aimed at the powerful's backside but at the head of the dispossessed.

The friend who returns takes his place in his family for a moment, which makes him react; first by denying it, then by recognizing it. On the other hand, the friend also goes out in search of friends after losing his family: he seeks to fill a void caused by a tragedy, and he does it through *substitution*.

When the father goes to ask his wife to marry her, she responds with an insult, which is almost a norm for this character played by Norma Aleandro. And later, at the end, the following dialogue unfolds, which does not bother anyone:

Father: "Where are we going for our honeymoon?"
Mother: "To hell."
Father: "I'll be by your side."
Mother: "What a drag."

Contrasts

Several contrasts will appear. Using photographic techniques, symbols will be reinforced:

The elderly couple in love is alternately shown with their son in the background, frantically talking on his cell phone. The calm and understanding words of the father contrast with the son's incomprehension and his vocabulary full of insults and outbursts.

When the three of them return to the nursing home, the mother says: "I won't leave your father here." After entering, her image is superimposed with the image of her son's face reflected in the glass door, which raises a question: it is not clear whether it is "logical" for the mother to be there or with her family, but at all times the blame is placed on "that illness" her mother suffers from: *the loss of memory*, which prevents her from living among others.

The celebration of the mother's birthday is done by the son and the father in the absence of the honoree, who still lives in the same city. This significant absence is multi-significant: the mother has died in some way, she is the past that has gone. Both toast with the best champagne while looking at an absence, saying: "Happy birthday, mommy." But, at the same time, the celebration is absurd, it lacks the subject, those who organized it have lost the meaning of the ceremony, not because of the mother's dementia but because of their own, which will be reversed, in part, towards the end, and begins to take shape at this very moment.

When the father reveals his intention to marry in church, the son questions him: "What happened to your principles[49], dad?"

---

[49] We must assume they are anticlerical, likely atheists.

Campanella makes satirical contrasts of the priest with his calculator. Also in the personification of the priest as an actor, as a professional of the spectacle, which will be presented twice: the first in the body of the priest doing sound checks with his speech; the second with the actor-priest, in the wedding staged for the mother.

Psychology

The protagonist, Rafael, will make his emotional conflicts explicit. The breakdown of the relationship with his mother—the mom, the protective grandma— as a result of his disobedience—abandoning his law degree— will leave a deep mark on him, on the son who is not recognized, not accepted by his mother. But the son will try to prove to her, at all costs, that he "is not useless," even though he did not become "*my son the doctor*"[50]. It will be of no use for his father to question this interpretation engraved in his conscious-unconscious: "Who told you that you were the useless one in the family?"

In this case, Rafael's conflict will be, above all, selfish but understandable: He needs his mother to recognize his worth, but she can no longer do so[51]. Nevertheless, he

---

[50] An allusion to the classic theatrical work of the same title by the Uruguayan playwright Florencio Sánchez.
[51] Rafael: —I opened the restaurant. Just when I could show her something I could do, she got sick.

insists on obtaining a sign of this recognition and what he gets is a confession: the mother also suffered the "lack of love" from her own mother[52].

This recognition is part of the lack, and Campanella will have other opportunities to express it differently. When the father proposes to his son his desire to marry in church with his mother, Rafael tells him it is madness, because she won't realize anything. If she doesn't realize it, it has no meaning, no value. To which the father confirms, "she will realize something, even if just a little." Even after the heart attack, when he seeks to make a change in his life, he again recognizes the importance of external recognition: "I worked so hard[53] to be someone and I have a restaurant that no one cares about."

Now, how is Rafael supposed to have tried to overcome this conflict, this lack of maternal recognition? Through obsessive work. An activity that not only prevented him from stopping to think—the desire and belief that he had to be involved in every detail of his business— but also that, in addition, would bring him success: "I've done much better than several professionals I know," says Rafael, which is not only a social reality in Argentina, but also a goal of the character who needs to compare himself to what he considers

---

[52] Mother: —Mom never calls me.
Rafael: —Did you remember Grandma?
Mother: —She doesn't love me.
[53] Distortion of the Italian word "laboro," very popular in Río de la Plata slang.

most important (a result of the maternal model). Now, in this desperate race to demonstrate that professional success that supposedly would fill the void, the protagonist needs to be alone. Others and their affections represent an obstacle in his competitive career. This is not only reflected in his relationship with his ex-wife but with everyone else. He proposes "more freedom" to his girlfriend, even though he loves her[54], and warns his daughter: "Don't be a pain in the neck[55] because I can't divorce you."

To maintain this mechanical order, even family relationships, fragmented by separations, divorces, misunderstandings, and new unions, must be structured like business: "Today is Thursday—, says the daughter—; it's my day with dad." Immediately after, and following a custody dispute, the father takes her away in a rush, with the same urgency he applies to his professional matters.

All the other characters, despite this family fragmentation, manage to rebuild new relationships. Even his girlfriend establishes a friendship with his daughter that he himself cannot achieve, and the same can be said of the new boyfriend or partner of his ex-wife[56].

---

[54] I think the way this proposal is presented isn't well resolved, but that's more about the formal execution of the script than the psychological analysis.

[55] A fundamental flaw of in-image translations is the failure to "represent" the spirit of Porteño language. There are crude simplifications that result in an absolute castration of the original expression.

[56] I'm not referring to a sex change. Probably the most accurate term would be *ex-wife*.

But the heart attack must serve as a dramatic wake-up call. It will mark a turning point in his life, which becomes evident as soon as he wakes up in the hospital bed. Then he acknowledges that one of his dreams is to "get the hell out of here."

That is his initial solution: faced with an unresolved conflict, he flees. Obsessive work was also a form of escape, which is why this is not the moment when he redirects his life. Going to Mexico to heal horses is more of a change in form than in substance.

But Rafael also flees from love. "Being in love is for kids."

His real change will come from within, when he reconsiders his romantic and family relationships.

Symbolism

I believe that in *El hijo de la novia* the symbolism is not forced, although this artistic possibility is not deeply explored either.

Certain recurrences of colors appear, such as blue walls always in contrast with some red female attire. Many of the garments are also blue, including the robe Rafael wears when he leaves his room (like a ghost carrying his own IV) and, when he turns around, he reveals his buttocks. The shirt he wears on other occasions is violet —that is, blue plus red—. The daughter's poetry notebook is also blue.

At the moment Rafael suffers the heart attack —a turning point in the plot and in the protagonist's life— he falls onto the portrait of his mother, which constitutes almost an allegory, a bit implausible but acceptable as a semiotic narrative. Later, he will wake up from his attack upon hearing his mother's voice calling him.

Upon Rafael's return after the attack, his friends welcome him with a heart-shaped cake and an arrow piercing it. Perhaps the most significant detail is the single candle that crowns it, which would symbolize a rebirth —although I believe this symbolism is not significant for the rest of the film.

More interesting is the assimilation of the vibrating phone —which is in the left pocket of Rafael's shirt— with a heart attack. At the same time, it serves to contrast with the silence of the church. Precisely, Campanella uses a very high shot in this space to emphasize the smallness of the man walking toward the altar.

When Rafael finally signs the sale of the restaurant, as he pulls out the contract paper, the camera stays with his image reflected on the glass table: his head is upside down, *inverted.* This device will be repeated when he returns to the restaurant for the last time: the chairs are all upside down, after the floors have been cleaned.

References to psychoanalysis are frequent. For example, when Rafael argues with his ex-wife, she tells him: "the index of Freud's works describes you." Rafael will also tell his girlfriend: "Take me to bed, but not to the couch." On the other hand, there will be constant allusions to therapies, etc.

However, I believe the most important symbolism in *El hijo de la novia* —and the one that structures an underlying plot— is the one referring to the saga of *El Zorro* 57, the avenger. He will appear repeatedly, starting from the children's game at the beginning, then in the world of adults, with frequent allusions to each character —such as Sergeant García, etc.—, or in the films that Rafael will watch alone during his moments of existential crisis.

El Zorro is a vigilante and, like all archetypes of the era, he is a loner —like El Llanero, etc.—. For this archetype, success and justice depend on a single man and, as if that weren't enough, it is possible.

Only the friend will turn to this story to contradict the positivist discourse of the childhood hero: "The fourteen-year-olds keep messing with the eight-year-olds." But Sergeant García has discovered the sad truth and, moreover, has been defeated: "I have no family, Rafael, but you do."

Even the secondary characters of *El Zorro* are repeated in *El hijo de la novia*: for example, when at the end Rafael —El Zorro, Don Diego— plays a prank on his friend —Sergeant García— by playing with his innocence: he confuses him with his ex-wife, lying to him that she was interested in the priest he was representing.

---

[57] North American series popular among children in the Río de la Plata region during the '60s and '70s.

Finally, Rafael makes a declaration-confession through the intercom —through a cold, blue image—. What he couldn't do without intermediaries, he does using the technology that once kept him enslaved.

Social and Historical Context

The relationship between history and memory is complex and conflictive in any society and, probably, even more so in Latin American societies like those of the Río de la Plata. Especially when their most recent histories are marked by the worst human rights violations that we couldn't see behind the Salvador Order.

What to remember and what to forget? Is it good to remember or does it only serve to tie us to the past? Until now, questions of this nature have never been considered in official and public discourse without a heavy dose of ideological bias. At times, the political left has used memory for its own vindication; on the other hand, the right —self-defined, not without reason, as the eternal "center"— has manipulated forgetting as a way to expand its sphere of economic domination, under the threat of a "return to disorder" that, contradicting the Brazilian flag, prevents us from achieving "progress." And in this race toward progress —systematically confused with the materialist model of the first world— everything is valid. *Even forgetting.*

As Marina Pianca aptly puts it58 "it's not just what we remember but what we do with that memory." Pianca then warns us that this ideology of forgetting —recognizable in postmodernity and, above all, with the meteoric rise of the legitimizers of power, of the current order, of the inevitable order, of the best of all possible worlds, like F. Fukuyama— is not new, but had already been warned about in 1966 by Ángel Rama59 under the name of "ideological appeasement."

In the case of the Río de la Plata, forgetting was organized by the political class and confirmed, in some way, by a large part of the population. In Argentina it was called "Punto Final," and included the classic pardon that is always reserved for wholesale criminals; in Uruguay there wasn't even the opportunity to initiate trials against human rights violators, as a prior amnesty law for the alleged subversives had to legitimize a subsequent amnesty for the military, which came with a law known as the Law of Impunity, which was confirmed by the population in a referendum that divided the country in two. 60 (which will surely be re-referendum in 2005, despite the legal-penal mechanism that practically denies this possibility).

---

58 The politics of dislocation (or return to the memory of the future).
59 Ángel Rama, Marcha Magazine, Montevideo, May 20, 1966.
60 Here too, we could apply the words of Marina Pianca: "Those who stubbornly continued to ask, to investigate, seemed marked as subversive archaeologists, grave robbers, or simply provocateurs." Pg. 130.

In *El hijo de la novia* this issue underlies the narrative, perhaps with greater force than the more current "economic crisis," which is also explicitly alluded to. Perhaps Norma Aleandro represents Argentina: that immigrant past, almost romantic, beautiful, that has fallen ill with forgetting. At the same time, her son —the Argentines— struggle to achieve recognition and do so through forgetting, without this mechanism being more effective than harmful. The discourse of success, as Pianca calls it, left a deep mark on Argentina in the 1990s, with its dream of already being in the "first world" —a promise made by President Carlos Saúl Menem—. It is necessary to forget in order to progress, to avoid conflict, the past. In El hijo de la novia, there is not only this conflict of memory-forgetting but also of tradition-modernity. Tradition —the family— is tinged with elements of American life, such as the close-up shots of Burger King and Coca-Cola. The novelty of the first world is the image of progress imposed by a dominant ideology, an ideology of success —I believe it was no minor symbolic detail the Menem government's obsession with maintaining the parity of 1 peso = 1 dollar, with sending its army to support the invasion of Iraq in 1991, etc.—; and it is, at the same time, forgetting as a prerequisite.

But "the past returns like a wave."

When a traffic officer stops him for driving while talking on the phone, Rafael will lie about a situation that justifies it (a woman's pregnancy). As is the norm, he will try to get out of it by using a "bribe." However, the bill he hands to the officer is fake, which the officer notices. The scene is a satirical but realistic portrayal of lying, simulation, and forgery, characteristics of Latin American societies and, perhaps especially, of the Argentine-Italian one.

As is common in Latin American cinema, the Church is a recurring theme and subject of satire. Some excellent dialogues use fine dialectics to contradict it.[61]

---

[61] When he is denied the possibility of his father marrying his mother due to her illness, the priest argues reasons of "discernment." To which Rafael responds: to be Catholic, you have to reason; but my mother wasn't reasoning when she was baptized. Of course, they had to secure new customers."

FRESA Y CHOCOLATE

Tomas Gutiérrez Alea, Cuba 1993.

The simultaneous consideration of *Memorias del subdesarrollo* and *Fresa y Chocolate*, by the same author, is entirely relevant, for several reasons. With just these two films, it is possible to get an idea of Tomas Gutiérrez Alea's cinema, his obsessions, and his evolution as a producer, director, and—surely—as a man. But it is also an embodied way of seeing the changes and social, psychological, and emotional processes of Cubans in the last third of the 20th century.

To begin with, the question is almost unavoidable: *how was such a film possible, in Cuba?*

In a certain scene, the protagonists listen to María Callas, and Diego, almost without double meanings, asks:

"Why doesn't the island produce a voice like that? With the need for *another voice*!"

And later:

"The only thing left is for them to ban children's songs."

So, how was such a film possible, in Cuba? Because, as I was able to confirm by talking to many Cubans, in different continents, politics or the Revolution is omnipresent in their thoughts. Which is a form of consciousness and, at times, of blindness62.

But these topics are not relevant now. Let's try to answer the initial question.

At the beginning of the 1990s, the global context had changed dramatically, especially for Cuba. Coupled with the growing economic difficulties that could weaken confidence in the Revolution and, above all, in its leaders, Cuba loses the financial and ideological (read "moral") support of the Soviet Union. Inflation rises along with the fiscal deficit. Production and consumption fall 63 It is then that the island must undertake changes, never radical but as dramatic as the circumstances warrant. Cuba must open up to overcome a crisis that threatens to sink it or to sink the Revolution.

But opening up also means, as much as possible, showing participation in the new times marked by feminism and growing sexual freedoms, for example. With an economy that takes refuge in tourism, the image must be one of greater tolerance towards diversity and the *other*. And this includes tolerance for cultural criticism.

But there are other factors that explain, in my view, the very fact of the making of this film and its approval by those

---

[62] "When will they understand that propaganda and art are not the same thing?" Diego, a character *from Strawberry and Chocolate.*
[63] *Fiscal dimension of Cuba's economic crisis,* 1986-1994, by Evaldo A. Cabarroury.

structures towards which the full weight of the moral consciousness that *Fresa y Chocolate* unleashes was directed. One is the undeniable prestige of its director, both within and outside of Cuba. Another is the fame garnered by the story *"El lobo, el bosque y el hombre nuevo"* by Senel Paz, which won the internationally renowned Juan Rulfo Prize. If we add to this the fact that this story had already become "the most photocopied" in Cuba's history, I believe there was little to gain from censorship and much to lose.

To confirm this, one need only look at what official outlets in Cuba said after the film's release:

> "A legitimate work of art that has quickly become indispensable, serving as a catalyst for unexpected social catharsis."

Revista Revolución y Cultura, Cuba.

> "*Fresa y chocolate* has the virtue of addressing a problem of our own, set in bygone years, and through which the filmmakers recreate their perspective to fulfill one of the oldest and most transcendent functions of art: to speak and critique, not to harm through irresponsible stone-throwing, but as an effective method to strive for self-improvement and to become better [...]"

Rolando Pérez-Betancourt, *Granma*, Havana, 1993

"If Titón wanted to make a film that would move and stir, he succeeded, and amidst the entertainment and seemingly easy jokes, the declaration of principles, the dignification of 'the others' fused in a friendly embrace, he earned the longest and warmest applause ever heard here [at the Havana Festival]." Raquel Peguero, La Jornada, Mexico City, 1993 "With its arrows aimed at all forms of intolerance, *Fresa y chocolate* arrives at a time when the collective consciousness of Cubans has matured and rejects elements that were attempted to be grafted onto it but never took root. [...] Those who see only a gay issue in the embrace of Diego and David are observing with a myopic gaze, or those who revel in their own trajectories and, by singing to the immediate tree, lose sight of the forest. Welcome this current moment of crisis if it promotes a reevaluation of the prevailing values in Cuban life and an irrefutable reaffirmation of national identity. In it, all flavors must have a place, that is, all options and interpretations."

Reynaldo González, "Cuban Culture with the Flavor of Strawberry and Chocolate," in Cuba, an Unfinished Assignment, Palma de Mallorca, 1998

"[...] more than a film for or against the system, the story has become an unparalleled lesson in learning that 'he who is not with me is not necessarily against me.' [...] *Fresa y chocolate* manages to rest its essential merit on the lucidity with which it approaches the context: critically, yes, but seeking to propagate its moral on much more ambitious and universal levels."

Juan Antonio García-Borrero: "Cuban Cinema: The Sleepless Eye," in *Memorias del cine cubano*, Casa de América, Madrid, 1999.

However, if we directly address the cinematic discourse, we might think that the film contains a strong critique of the officialist structure on which these very media outlets depend. Even the critique is directed at the same discourses that were disseminated and supported by these outlets, sometimes with critical judgment, but at other times in the image and likeness of *Pravda* (Truth[64]). A critique that denounces, I believe explicitly, the degradation of the Revolution into ideological dogmatism, the official discourse as unquestionable Revelation, as an act of faith, frozen and repetitive, reminiscent of historical periods dominated by religious discourse and control, so despised by Marxism itself. It is no coincidence that an important intellectual like Julio García Espinosa spoke, in 1969, of the "Revolution" with a capital R, as a fervent Christian might speak of the Crucifixion or the Gospels. ("The Revolution has liberated us as an artistic sector," he wrote at the time.)

Now let us briefly examine some formal and thematic aspects of *Fresa y Chocolate*.

---

[64] Even in our ideological regions, there were (and still are) media outlets with pharisaical titles like "La Razón," etc., and no less dogmatic than the famous Soviet newspaper.

If we pause to consider the creative personality of To-mas Gutiérrez Alea, we will find in this film some recurring themes: for example, the critical observation of the urban neglect of Havana, present in *Memorias del subdesar-rollo*, which reflects not only economic decline but also the Revolution's negligence toward the city, in "favor" of agricultural reforms and their supposed greater importance (what Alvin Toffler would call the First Wave).

We also encounter the theme of exile as an ethical prob-lem once again. Vivian (again, a woman[65]) leaves for Italy. But her journey-escape is not motivated by ethical or ideo-logical reasons, but rather by personal motives, more re-lated to unscrupulous selfishness than to a vindication of the individual[66]. Here we once again have the selfish, fraud-ulent woman: the refined prostitute, the high-class prosti-tute who not only sells her body but—what is worse—her conscience, her soul. The same happens with Sergio's wife, the protagonist of *Memories of Underdevelopment.*

Different, however, is the case of Diego, the "new moral hero." Diego leaves "because he is expelled," because

---

[65] There is, however, a female character who represents the new ethic, which is, in fact, of ancient Christian origin, but which after 380 A.D. ended up being denied and refuted by "Institutional" Christianity. This is the case of "the prostitute," Diego's friend: "Inside me, there is some-thing no one could soil." This means: *She has sold her body, but not her soul,* which puts her at an advantage compared to Vivian, the woman who has sold her soul for thirty pieces of silver.

[66] "I wanted to live well, dress well, now that I'm young..." says Vivian, justifying her marriage to a man she did not love.

he has been denied a right that is inherent to every human being, according to the new rules beginning to take root in the ethical consciousness of society. But he leaves after a long, also heroic, *struggle for principles*. Diego is, then, the new "revolutionary," the new martyr. And it is important to note that, in this sense as well, there is a notable, radical change: the one who leaves is not a traitor, but a victim.[67] A victim of a system, of a bureaucracy, and of individuals who, like Miguel, remain clinging to a dogmatic, sexist, and entirely prejudiced discourse, according to the new ethics, to the point of demonstrating their materialist dialectic with phrases like:

"Do you think you can trust a guy who doesn't defend his own sex?"

This is countered by the new ethics (by the "new man"):

"Aren't you afraid it might have some ideological effect on you? says Diego, after inviting David with a glass of the "enemy's drink."[68]

Further proof that the film focuses primarily on *a struggle for ethics*—or on a struggle between different ethics— can be seen when, at another moment, Miguel argues, to trap the queer:

"This isn't a problem with the police. It's a political and moral problem."

---

[67] "Reality (...) is a cultural and not a natural matter," Mas'ud Zavarzaeh
[68] whisky

And later, Miguel insists, categorically, with the force-fulness and eloquence of the foolish:

"The Revolution doesn't enter through the ass."

Also repeated in *Strawberry and Chocolate*, as in *Memories of Underdevelopment*, is the need for circularity, so common in much of Latin American narrative. The film closes almost the same way it opens, repeating the same scene. But it is a repetition with a powerfully significant variation: *a transformation has occurred* in the initiatory journey: when, at the end, the characters go to have ice cream, they repeat the scene where they first met, but this time they exchange roles[69]. In between, there has been a revelatory experience, equivalent to a profound reflection. The transformation through revelation has an ethical value, and perhaps this is one of the fundamental pillars that gives meaning to *Strawberry and Chocolate*.

Another repetition, perhaps not as significant, refers to the double standard—or the accusation of falsity—that falls on the Cuban woman, a general symbol of a supposed "Latin American society."

I believe that, revisiting the enthusiastic parallel drawn by Julio García Espinosa, when comparing the Latin American Literary Boom with the New Latin American Cinema, we can appreciate a characteristic that differentiates them almost radically and, for that very reason, mysteriously

---

[69] "The only flaw is that you're not gay" / "Well, nobody's perfect"

unites them: While the so-called "Boom" of Latin American Literature was associated—albeit imprecisely—with "magical realism," the New Latin American Cinema, on the other hand, has been linked from its beginnings to today with its opposite, that is, with Italian "neorealism." With the exception—my vast ignorance allows me to name only one case—of films like *Like Water for Chocolate* and, with the exception of the scene in *Strawberry and Chocolate* where they carry a live pig up a staircase, which is surreal, humorous, or loaded with symbolic connotations I was unable to decipher.

I believe that *Strawberry and Chocolate* subscribes to a tradition: the art of protest. And it does so to the extent that it is capable—and, moreover, intends—to understand art as a synthesis of ethics and aesthetics. I deeply believe that there is a distinct emotional value in this combination that does not exist in pure aesthetics or in ethical reflection in its pure state.

The paradox, perhaps, lies in the fact that this "type of art" was predominantly a characteristic of artists and intellectuals vaguely and imprecisely labeled as "left-wing," who resonated with a broad audience when Latin America was submerged in the dictatorships of the sixties, seventies, and eighties. In *Strawberry and Chocolate* this particular form of art turns against its own origin. Or, if we go beyond the surface, we should say that it rescues its own roots.

LA VIRGEN DE LOS SICARIOS

Fernando Vallejo and Barbet Schroeder.

Where There Are No Innocents

It is the form of love that Vallejo knows and that keeps a dying society half-alive, a society that needs to attack in order to confirm itself as an existing being that fears dissolving into fiction, dreams, or madness, without realizing that it already has.

Fernando Vallejo, screenwriter of the film Our Lady of the Assassins and author of the novel of the same name, defined it with these revealing words: "it is a love story in the country of hate"[70]

However, I will take the liberty of contradicting the author himself, based on an undeniable fact: the author is the main character, the eyes and the conscience of the cinematic narrative. But I am not referring merely to the fact that the protagonist of *Our Lady of the Assassins* —the writer— is Vallejo's "alter ego". I am referring to something more: Fernando Vallejo is a significant part of that Colombia that is reflected, with all its lights and all its shadows, in

---

[70] Also, in Madrid, Fernando Vallejo wanted to clarify: "The film is not a sociological documentary, but a love story set in Medellín"

his own film. When Vallejo denies Colombia, he confirms it; when he despises it, he flatters it; when he destroys it, he reconstructs it.

To realize this, if we want to delve into Colombian reality and, above all, into the reality of *Our Lady of the Assassins*, let us mention aspects of Fernando Vallejo's personality.

"We must kill President Andrés Pastrana," said Vallejo on a Colombian radio station. Later he clarified: "I don't feel that I am crazy. What I feel is a great chaos in my head"

This is how we must understand this "love" story, and this is how we must understand when, from the beginning, Alexis presents his credentials to the audience with an expression that is an oxymoron representative of Colombian chaos:

"[They were] in love with hate."[71]

And almost immediately:

"We were born to die."

But before entering the film, let us briefly return to Vallejo:

"I insult repeatedly to see who will kill me," he said once. "And, as everything in Colombia, it will remain in

---

[71] This impossible pair becomes evident when the protagonist "falls in love" and takes to bed a young man who turns out to be the killer of his former lover, whom he forgives. (This expression "they loved each other with hatred" is repeated in another Latin American film).

confusion. For Colombia to kill me is an honorable way to escape the horror of life."[72]

So far his desires. But there are more revelations. Let us see, for example, his philosophy of existence:

"A man is a biological machine programmed to ejaculate and everything else is hypocrisy, chatter, stories"

This "biological machine programmed to ejaculate" is the same one that, in the initial scene, when Alexis lies down with the writer —with Vallejo—, walks with an automatic pistol[73] in the place where his penis should be. The translation is too obvious: man is a biological machine programmed to ejaculate... bullets.

That is to say —and always based on that philosophy of existence—, man is a machine, not for life, but for death. Being born does not give pleasure (we are always born crying); pleasure comes from killing and dying (in sex we "kill" and "die"). Everything else is hypocrisy.

And perhaps for that very reason there are practically no female characters in *Our Lady of the Assassins,* not even for sex. Because woman is also a biological machine from the same cosmogony—, but programmed to give life.—

"Sin is to keep giving birth," says the writer almost at the end.

---

[72] The protagonist returns to Medellín to die, according to his own words. Although he does not succeed in the ninety-seven minutes the film lasts, he uses that time to make it clear that what interests him most is doing so. "I don't want to live anymore —he says later—. I'm living overtime"

[73] "El tote" or "fierro."

When a woman screams in fear upon witnessing a murder —as the last glimmer of humanity echoing in those cold, yellow streets—, the writer approaches to comment, always with irony:

"What's wrong, ma'am? We're not in Switzerland," and then he mocks: "There are no innocents; everyone is guilty." That is, everyone must die, or it doesn't matter if they are killed.

The woman who appears the most is Alexis's mother, after her son has died, and her appearance shows her surrounded by children, like the reproduction machine she is, with the only exception being that she gets paid to have them and to lose them.[74] At this moment, almost at the end, this woman's children are all boys. They are no older than childhood, and the first words they utter in this world refer to the murder of someone who has not yet died.

The very title of the film alludes to a woman —who is also sacred, according to tradition—, a source of miracles that the protagonists seek repeatedly in churches. Perhaps

---

[74] Why does the writer go to the maternal home of his deceased lover? Probably so that the woman can confirm the wickedness of men (the husbands who abandoned her). However, this confirmation would add nothing to the film. Instead, the money the woman receives from the lover —and destroyer— of her son is entirely significant: she, too, the woman, is a "producer," albeit of life (the children), and she must be paid for it, it is necessary to degrade the little that remains sacred in that cursed city, according to Vallejo. It is no longer enough to kill the fruit of her womb; she must also be degraded in the name of compassion.

there are as many scenes showing virgins[75], church interiors (the womb), as there are streets and dead bodies.

The Virgin of the Assassins is an attempt to organize chaos[76]. The protagonist is not only a writer (the contemporary witness, the cursed prophet), but also a "grammarian." "The last grammarian," as he first said, and "the first grammarian," as he later said, while his lover fired three or four shots at an illiterate man —we can presume.

The grammarian is the one who orders the symbols; the grammarian is not as interested in content as in form. Where a sign reads "NO DUMPING OF CORPSES," that's where the most corpses are piled up. "Surely people come up here to dump corpses where it's forbidden."

The grammarian prays in churches, almost obsessively, while asking Jesus to kill Wilmar, his new lover. The grammarian kneels before the Virgin and then, in bed, declares:

"Blessed be Satan, in the absence of God..."

And almost at the end:

"God needs us to exist" —a worn-out but significant phrase in the mouth of a pilgrim.

Later, further on, he states that turning the other cheek only promotes impunity. The path is another. Not justice, but revenge. Repeated death, even if it means praying to

---

[75] "Santa Anita" is also a music machine, a "woman-machine" from the protagonist's deepest past.
[76] In an initial scene, the protagonist asks what time it is, standing in front of a wall where many clocks hang, each showing a different time.

the Virgin and asking the Son. The protagonist reclaims revenge against impunity. However, if something character-
izes the actions of these characters —and much of
Colombian society— it is, precisely, their chilling *impunity*.

There will also be biblical references, on one hand, and
confirmations of the emptiness of meaning in form, as in
the allusions to the smell of marijuana in a church and the
sale of condoms in the same religious space.[77]

Now, we know that the protagonist, the writer, is the
alter ego of Fernando Vallejo, who represents him in body
and soul[78]. Therefore, it would be difficult to claim that
there was, in the making of this film, the intention to ex-
press/denounce the hypocrisy of part of Colombian society
through this character. Every cursed ego that, throughout
the history of art, philosophy, and literature, has always
sought to present itself as amoral, immoral, and even "anti-
moral" —even as cynical—, has never been able to bear the
idea of being labeled a "hypocrite." However, the result is
the same: the writer does not position himself as a critic or
accuser of the hypocrisy and corruption of his society, because he himself embodies those attributes of Colombian
society that he loves and hates. He hates the poor more than
poverty[79]. Almost as nostalgic as the tango, the protagonist

---

[77] The merchants whom Jesus expelled from the temple (a common practice among the Hebrews at the beginning of our era).
[78] In his passions, his obsessions, and his conception of life.
[79] "Put two poor people together, and they will produce ten poor people.
I hate poverty." The protagonist's protest is also repeated when he is

returns in search of his origins to die. He longs for a past that, in reality, was likely no better nor any more innocent than the present.

"Before, we settled things with machetes," says the writer; "now with lead."

When his young lover asks him to buy him a gun, the writer almost convinces us of his good intentions:

"I'm against all violence," he says.[80]

Even when Alexis kills the first taxi driver, he almost manages to convince us that he is horrified by the act. Until we eventually realize that, in reality, his young lovers carry out the dirty work that he himself does not want to perform but deliberately provokes.[81]

The Virgin of the Hitmen is the expression of that chaos that reveals itself in a permanent state of anguish, dissatisfaction, and deafening noises. In turn, these noises (the

---

given half a paper napkin instead of a whole one, which causes him noticeably more annoyance than he shows for a man murdered in the street.

[80] "Don't you distinguish between thought and action?"— he seems to reproach the young man when he kills the hippie who had been bothering them at night with his drumming.— What lies between one and the other is called civilization."

[81] Often, this false innocence is reflected in dialogues like the following:
P_1: —Four million souls sleep [in the night of Medellín]. There are no crimes, no one kills anyone.
P_2: —Not at all. That's when it gets good.
Later, when the young lover runs out of bullets, it is he himself who gets them from the police, which also brings us back to the contradiction between discourse and action (protagonist/police).

violence) are a way to silence the "funereal silence" that follows each murder[82]

Faithful to the ancient Aristotelian precept of art as unity, *The Virgin of the Assassins* achieves its own through various strategies, ranging from the narrative thread of a single protagonist to the repetition of a monochrome based on the color yellow[83], including the repeated intention to assault the senses[84].

If this is a nihilistic story,[85] it is a kind of nihilism that does not recognize pleasure without one's own suffering or that of others. It is the form of love that Vallejo knows (paid or unpaid) and that keeps a dying society half-alive, a society that needs to aggress in order to confirm itself as an

---

[82] "There's a buzzing,"— complains the writer, sleepless, as he no longer hears the murdered drummer.— It must be the sound of conscience." Seven nights of funereal silence have followed.

[83] Yellow, obviously, represents Colombia and Bolívar. But it can also be associated with illness and death. The taxis are yellow— (which are so abundant in the film),— the buses, the candles in the churches, the awnings in the squares, the facades of old buildings, the marquees, Alexis's jacket and clothes, the telephone, etc.

[84] The loud music in the apartment and in the taxi drivers' radios, the frantic way they drive...

[85] Near the end, the tango is heard: Yira: "When the batteries are dead/ of all the doorbells/ that you press/ looking for a fraternal chest/ where to die burned/ when they leave you stranded/ after cinching/ the same as me/ when you notice that by your side/ they try on the clothes/ that you will leave/ You'll see that everything is a lie/ you'll see that nothing is love/ that the world cares for nothing... (the other tango that is heard is Volver and, of course, it refers to the protagonist's journey). On the other hand, the protagonist himself repeats: "Everything is unreal," or elsewhere: "If you're not on TV, you don't exist."

existing being that fears dissolving into fiction, dreams, or madness, without realizing that it already has.

The protagonist himself acknowledges this when he tells his young lover:

"*Boy*, you will never be able to know happiness."[86]

The Virgin of the Hitmen an attempt to organize chaos, and its final image—the image of the most terrible Colombia—is a morgue where secretaries, desks with computers, and all the necessary bureaucratic apparatus have been installed (if these two words ever did not form an oxymoron) to organize the greatest institution of Colombian society: premature death.

As is often the custom, the final song is not chosen at random:

Amorcito
that lost its nest
Without finding shelter
In the storm...

In some way, Fernando Vallejo is the cursed, dirty, confused, and lucid conscience of Colombian society. He is the dream or the accusatory nightmare that torments the criminal. An artist in the deepest sense of the word—even if he does not want to be. And The Virgin of the Assassins is the synthesis of both: the current social order of Colombia and

---

86 When Wilmar writes on a napkin what he desires in life, though it is a common critique of postmodern consumer society, the boy writes: famous brand clothes (Calvin Klein), a motorcycle, a refrigerator...

Vallejo himself, which is to say, perhaps, the same thing. Both will disappear—as the main character announces, in different ways—, because it is natural and necessary.

According to Brodwell[87], classical Hollywood narrative presents us with "psychologically defined" individuals who struggle to solve a well-defined problem. And it is the *causality* that revolves around the character or characters that provides the fundamental unifying principle, while spatial configurations are motivated by realism.

In *The Virgin of the Hitmen you* can recognize some of these principles barely confirmed. At times we will see spaces—generally urban or suburban areas of Medellín—treated with realism, or with that intention of approaching the social paradigm of a human group at a specific moment in history, which we call "realism." But we will also find dream-like spaces[88] reflecting, at times, impossibilities, such as a flying motorcycle, or improbabilities, such as a stream of rainwater that turns into or mixes with a stream of blood.

If we take this stream of blood as (1) a fact that aims to be "real," then we are referring to the fantastic, the unreal; but (2) if we take it as an unreal fact, for example, a reflection of the feverish psychology of the protagonist, we are

---

[87] *New Concepts in Film Theory*, Robert Stam, Robert Burgoyne, Sandy Flitterman-Lewis. Ed. Piados 1999. Page 216.

[88] As is the case with the facade of a church that the protagonist discovers in his dreams before, supposedly, he does so in waking life (the latter understood as "reality").

referring to a kind of realism or hyperrealism, since a narrative that involves the physical world as well as the psychological and spiritual world should be "more real," that is, the stones and the dreams about the stones. A world made only of stones would be a fantastic world, as it presupposes the absence of that which gives it phenomenological—if not ontological, also—to those "physical" objects: the gaze, human perception. That is to say, even the most scientific materialism remains an intellectual construct. At times, a impoverished version of reality. Hence, these paradoxes, which feed back into each other, relativize to an extreme the qualification of "real space"[89]

I believe, instead, that we could take a simpler and more direct path by recalling another definition by Bazin, for whom that "impression of reality" in classical cinema is due to more specific categories: editing practices, camera and sound work, the reconstruction of a fictional world characterized by (a) internal coherence, (b) linear causality, (c) psychological realism, and (d) temporal and spatial continuity[90]. All are categories that we can apply to *The Virgin of the Assassins*. In it, there are no visual movements in which the camera takes on significant protagonism; the

---

[89] Especially considering that we did not put on the table the possibility of a symbolism that is not related to either the psychology (inner world) of the character or the physical world (outer world).

[90] What for Barthes would be the *legible text*, of the classical text. *New Concepts in Film Theory*, Robert Stam, Robert Burgoyne, Sandy Flitterman-Lewis. Ed. Piados 1999. Page 219.

music often recalls classical Hollywood cinema (emphasis on the sinister, etc.). There is causality —the characters kill and die according to a "logical" sequence[91]—; the psychology of the characters is entirely plausible[92] and the spatial and temporal continuities are ensured at all times. There is no intention, as in Brecht, to oppose one moment to another, to disconnect it. Each scene complements the others. Nor is there what this same playwright would call "reflexivity"[93], that "principle by which art must reveal the principles of its own construction, to avoid fraud" [94]

The theory that cinema is intrinsically realistic, since its means of reproduction ensure "objectivity," since the cinematic process implies an identical link between the photographic analogue and its referent, because it lacks —unlike painting, for example— the possibility of not working with

---

[91] "He didn't deserve to die, he was a criminal"; "He had to die because he made too much noise"; "I killed him because he had killed my brother," etc.

[92] Jorge Luis Borges, referring to the "psychological novel," said that there are no improbable characters. In other words, one could understand that there are no unreal psychologies. Within sanity and madness lies the infinite universe of ways of being.

[93] A notable example of "artistic reflexivity," in my opinion, is Ernesto Sábato's total novel *Abaddon the Exterminator* (Buenos Aires, 1974)

[94] Op. cit., pg. 225.

real models[95], is entirely arbitrary and naive and can be re-futed with scenes like these last ones[96].

As for the characters, one could say they are "psycho-logically defined," though this should not be taken as "psy-chologically healthy." The same could be said of that other set of characters who interact to form "Colombian society," or the "urban society of Medellín." Their psychological traits are well defined, *not despite* their dramatic contradic-tions *but precisely because of them*.

On the other hand, *The Virgin of the Assassins* com-pletely defies the first principle of classical Hollywood nar-rative, as defined by Bordwell, since we will not find in this film —at least not in the first readings— a struggle of the individual for a "clearly defined" goal. On the contrary, I believe that one of the narrative foundations of the film lies in this very lack of purpose in the characters. At all times, the writer and his lovers get in and out of taxis. It doesn't matter so much where they are going, but what, con-sciously or unconsciously, happens during the journey: the

---

[95] This point is definitively refuted by the latest cinematic practices, where characters and landscapes have been replaced by virtual construc-tions.

[96] When Galileo popularized the telescope, many people saw through that instrument an "objective reality": they saw the Earth as the center of the Universe. Some saw the destiny of men and women in the same zo-diac signs that the ancients used to see the same thing. Others even saw that the Sun was the center of the planetary system, which we also know is not true —if we look at the System from an interior point, we will see another "reality," no less "real": the Sun revolves around that point.

blare of the radio, the hallucinatory way of driving, the challenge, the provocation, the defiance, and finally, the elimination of the subject who represents the assassins themselves. The same happens in their repeated pilgrimages to churches: there isn't even a religious purpose, which increases the contradiction and —even more— the confirmation of the lack of meaning, of purpose. Another element that seems to confirm this idea is the dialogues:

"And now what do we do?"

"I don't know. Shall we go out into the street again?"

This mechanism is supported by an *ad hoc* that only serves the plot: the writer has received an inheritance and has a great deal of money at his disposal. In this way, it is possible to throw music equipment out the window, with satisfaction on both sides[97], only to buy a new set later. The same goes for the destruction of the television by Alexis, with shots fired at the image of a president they cannot kill[98]. It is not an *ad hoc*, however, that the apartment[99] where the protagonists live is empty —that is, *lacking content*. The apartment is empty and, frequently, is filled with

---

[97] Once again, we notice the same psychological formula: *destruction provokes pleasure*. Man is a machine programmed to ejaculate, destroy, kill. Then it will be necessary to find a substitute to destroy again. Destruction confirms the subject who destroys, but, in the end, the destroyer, the killer, seeks his own death at the hands of the other. "I want Colombia to kill me"

[98] "We must kill the president...", said Fernando Vallejo.

[99] Apartment: dwelling, life, interior, intimacy, morality, self-confession. Perhaps even Colombia.

blaring *rock*[100] music; it is as empty as the meaning of the religious ritual in the churches, as the lives of the protagonists themselves, who, from time to time, draw back some curtains to see Medellín[101].

This does not mean that there is no purpose in the writer's return to his hometown. In fact, it is difficult, if not impossible, to find human behavior devoid of purpose. This would negate psychoanalysis at its root and the universe of religions[102]. It would also turn *The Virgin of the Assassins* into an accident —contingency— that is almost impossible.

If *The Virgin of the Assassins* still subscribes to neorealism, we could say that it also possesses neoclassical elements in its unity of time, space, and action —or inaction. At times, time flows at different speeds, but there are no ambiguities in the passage of linear time, and the narrative itself aims to make this clear with details, for example, of

---

[100] Could it be an *overinterpretation* to link this *rock* music with North America?

[101] It is the same act of going out into the street, alternately and without purpose, to see the city, though also to contribute to its destruction.

102 I would even deny Sartre's existentialism, since while in this case all human existence might lack purpose —meaning—, no human act lacks purpose, as it is immersed in a sea of meanings. For Sartre, there were no "hidden feelings" —a Freudian unconscious, for example—, because it is not possible to feel something one does not know: *to know is to feel*. But, even so, only the movement of stones and the growth of trees would lack purpose (as long as Darwin does not appear to deny it, of course).

the writer's beard and the dialogues, which confirm certain dates.

We can also find what Bazin calls[103] "transparency," that is, the intention of the cinematic production to "erase all traces" that remind the viewer they are watching a film. In other words, any "distraction" of consciousness or analysis that pulls the viewer out of the state of *reverie* and identification produced by the hypnosis of cinema. By erasing the "work of the film," the "vague, untheorized world" would be reproduced. In other words: the dominant ideology would be reproduced.

This last concept is one I would prefer to call "boomerang."[104] Probably this "vague and untheorized world" is reproduced in a "vague and untheorizing audience," that is, in a "consumerist and uncritical" audience. Living in a garbage dump can help perpetuate unhygienic habits. However, the decontextualized exposure —through art— of the same garbage dump will provoke rejection rather than assimilation[105]. To put it in a less graphic example, cinema and art in general can, to some extent, present machismo, racism, or the domination of an economically

---

103 *New Concepts in Film Theory*, Robert Stam, Robert Burgoyne, Sandy Flitterman-Lewis. Ed. Piados 1999. Page 215.

104 Similar to the concept of "Deconstruction," as a critical, perhaps hermeneutic activity.

105 This type of narration would fall within what Barthes called *writable text*. What for Barthes would be the *legible text*, of the classical text. *New Concepts in Film Theory*. Page 219.

superior class as a "natural" way of being in a society, repro-
ducing its rules of oppression. However, the abstraction of
that same nature and its *amplification* or *repetition* will have
an inverse result: by emphasizing one fact *those other facts or
rules that justify it are lost*. Or they no longer appear as necessary or natural, but as *responsible*. It is at this moment,
then, that the "innocent" camera ceases to be a weapon of
domination and becomes a weapon of critique, that is, of
"liberation."

   In the previous essay, *Where There Are No Innocents*,
I emphasized the author's personality to explain, in part,
my reading of *The Virgin of the Assassins*. At the same time
as the "I" as an individual and creator, I wanted to present
Vallejo as a representative of Colombian culture —partly
involved in his critique of it, as both victim and responsible—.106 For Foucault, the future would be characterized
by a generalized anonymity of discourse. That is, the author
not as the traditional source of the work of art but as a kind
of medium. Personally, I believe that historically both have
occurred: there has never been a "creator" without society
or a work of art without an author. Even when the authors

---

106 *La virgen de los sicarios* is not a "dominant film," nor one of "resistance," as Commolli and Narboni might classify it (Idem., pg. 224). Perhaps it is both things at the same time or, better, perhaps we could place
it within the term "rupture film," from the same authors, since superfi-
cially it belongs to dominant or traditional cinema —at least in its form,
in the author's declaration of intent not to make a "sociological" film but
a film that tells a "love story"— but in which a fissure opens in its internal
critique.

were a group, it has always been a minority group that reflected society itself or attacked it with different values —new—. However, even in this change, in this aggression, the individual and society as a whole were also interacting. The actor has not died, nor has the reader been born[107]. Both have always been there, only in diverse forms, in different proportions. In constant change.

The Virgin of the Assassins did not arise by spontaneous generation; nor would it have been the same result if the author had been Pablo Escobar or Andrés Pastrana. That is, the author is never a minor detail, a means of saying something that "naturally" must be said by a certain society. But neither is the author a superior subject, indifferent to that society: their creative action is motivated and, probably, justified within it.

---

[107] Barthes.

ROJO AMANECER

Jorge Fons, Xavier Robles, and Guadalupe Ortega, 1989

In Search of the Lost Tlatelolco

Surely the events of Tlatelolco (October 2, 1968) deserved a better film than Rojo Amanecer. Not because something "beautiful" can be made of a massacre, but because, at times, art manages to elevate and dignify the victims of an injustice and, through them, humanity as a whole. In this sense, Rojo Amanecer adds nothing.

However, I believe its greatest value —though not artistic— is its documentary —sociological— nature, that kind of fiction or *reconstruction* of history without pretensions of objectivity.

But is it a "documentary"? No, it is not a simple chronological ordering of events, with pretensions of objectivity or "historical truth." *Rojo Amanecer* is much more than that: it is the narration of historical events from the perspective of a Mexican family that could have lived through them. And, through this, there is not only a "reconstruction" of events but also a critical characterization of the society that was both victim and participant in the massacre[108].

However, *Rojo Amanecer* is not an *interrogative* work but an "explanatory" one (and here lies its documentary profile). It does not aim to question but to present its version of the events and, —as if that were not enough—, it makes an ethical evaluation in their presentation.

Personally, I do not disagree with the "version" of the events presented in *Rojo Amanecer*. Not even with its moral perspective on society. But in my view, the best works of art belong to the first group, to those works that are capable of *interrogating* before *answering* or attempting to induce the *truth* of the events. Generally, interrogative works radiate a plurality of readings (they are "open works," as Humberto Eco would say).

Symbolism

From this perspective —of the vindicatory discourse—, *Rojo Amanecer* is entirely predictable.

---

[108] "After this massacre —says one of the students, at the end— the people must do something. The people cannot leave us alone." In some way, the film wants to say that the people *will* leave them alone, which is a constant in our societies: the attitude of looking the other way, of not getting involved with the pain of others. This same attitude will fall upon the same "idealistic students," when, almost at the end, a mother searches for her son shouting. Upon realizing that there is no one among them with the name the woman is shouting, they go back to sleep.

The very ambiguity of its title "Rojo Amanecer" alludes to the bloodshed at dawn and the emergence of a probable leftist insurrection.

At times, its characters are also predictable and, what could be worse, they are stereotyped. It does not quite reach the status of a "work of art," from my personal perspective, because it presents a discourse that is sufficiently closed, symbolically repeated, and worn out, so that, by the end of the film, the viewer leaves with a new vision of an old problem.

Let us try to clarify this point.

The reading of *Rojo Amanecer* is heavily directed. Even the technical strategies it uses, its symbolism, is very direct, bordering on the allegorical. For example, the clocks. Clocks are everywhere, just in case.

From the beginning, the sound of the "tick-tock" of an alarm clock fills every space the camera moves through. This resource, which is not at all bad, as a soundscape and as symbolism, has a very direct reading: something is about to happen. Something important, something grave. All the events that follow will only be preludes to it. The "tick-tock" has the unsettling force of a *time bomb*.

Now, where is the evil? There is no doubt: in the government. The government is the superior, invisible, perverse, and unreachable —*Kafkaesque* entity. It fills everything. Its hand, like that of God or the hand of (in)justice, reaches everyone. Its destruction, like that of Lucifer, is incontestable.

The mother: —You don't mess with the government. How many dead are there already, how many disappeared?

For the mother, the government is not unjust: *it is the scourge of nature.*

It will be she herself who, while cleaning or rummaging through her children's bedroom, will find a subversive magazine that says:

"Why is this the truth?"

The symbolism of this discovery is twofold. On the one hand, the magazine is obscene, and the mother's gesture of discovering a pornographic magazine in her son's room is the same. On the other hand, the title of the publication recalls certain religious magazines, deeply proselytizing, such as "Awake!" or "The Watchtower," so popular in the Hispanic world, which also refer to the discovery of the Truth. All of this is accompanied by various icons, such as the image of Che Guevara —competing in size and position with the image of Jesus109 in the other spaces—, turning the room into a kind of "atheist chapel."

---

109 The symbolic relationship between Jesus and Che Guevara is evident, and we will expand on it further in later essays. As if that were not enough, their ethical valuation is the same. I would say that Che Guevara is profoundly Christian, in this sense: he is the bearded martyr, the one who dies to save others. Above all, he is the subversive —like Jesus, of course— who at times stands alone against the full weight of power. Che Guevara is betrayed by a Bolivian shepherd and assassinated. In this sense, the account of the soldier who must kill him is revealing. From my

Perhaps this last scene is one of the most successful in *Rojo Amanecer.*

A second "spatial transmigration," if I may use the term,— occurs when the grandfather, the captain, hears the tanks: then his face appears as if made up for war camouflage. It is war, the nostalgia for times of action, when he was useful, powerful. After all, war is to a soldier what the stage is to a theater actor:—*his vocation.*

Another achievement, I think, is the moment when the *meeting*[110] begins. Outside, dramatic voices and whistles are heard. It is an event, if only for the number of attendees. However, the camera never shows anything resembling the massive gathering of apolitical[111] event. It only reflects it in

---

perspective, the executioner was aware of that "Christ-like" image, an unarmed prisoner, before whom he was moved before pulling the trigger. He was not just a guerrilla, the object of all his hatred, but a mythical figure. The physical stature of the condemned man alone impressed the soldier. From that moment on, Che's followers will undoubtedly engage in a proselytism that is both mythical and mystical, no different from that carried out by the early Christians in the catacombs of Cappadocia or Rome, paying for it with their lives.

[110] A paradoxical way to name a "demonstration" or "gathering" of groups that are supposed to be, for the most part, leftist, that is, anti-Yankee.

[111] One could argue that the production was poor. However, not much more is needed to capture images of crowds. On the contrary, I believe that intuition here led to the achievement of an economy of expressive means, as can be seen in some of Hitchcock's films, such as *Rear Window* (1954?), for example.

the faces of the children looking out the window[112]. And, above all, I find that the greatest symbolic and ethical value of this scene lies in the attitude of the characters inside the apartment: they do not want to see, they want to deliberately disengage——something that will prove impossible for them— and, like the mother or the grandfather, they try to prevent the others from looking, from seeing, from being interested in what is happening.

The obedient grandson: —The *meeting* is about to start

The grandfather: —What do you know about *meetings*. Get away from that window!

(The obedient grandson starts doing his homework)

Other symbolisms are not as interesting, overused and almost laughable. For example, the repeated display of portraits of Jesus. Not to mention the moment when the gunfire that was killing people below ends up entering through a window to directly hit the image of the Crucified. As if that weren't enough, and as if the intention hadn't been understood, almost at the end one of the students will walk through the room and spend long seconds looking at the symbolic crime, the desecration by the wicked.

"In these times, it's more dangerous to be a student than a criminal," says one of the protagonists and prepares to burn his ID. This does not constitute a great phrase,

---

[112] The grandfather: "I'm busy," he says, pretending to fix a clock (a gift from an old General) while his daughter knits nervously. Later, the obedient grandson will say: "There are lights in the sky; like in the movies."

much less a great thought. But it sets the stage for some interesting images: the burning of IDs, which are then thrown into the toilet. Also, the burning of "propaganda" recalls the "burning of books," characteristic of periods of state intolerance. However, it's not clear why the portrait of Che Guevara remains until the end, defiant on a wall, to condemn the rebellious children, as if the filmmakers hadn't wanted to find a more plausible way to provoke the bloody final scene.

In the analysis of the film's symbolic resources, this entire battery of allegories and direct messages is evident, which at times border on naivety, casting *Rojo Amanecer* in a light of implausibility. The same goes for the performances: they are overacted, especially in the final scenes[113]. But if we go back to the Middle Ages, we'll find that this need for "allegorization" and "overacting" was a rule[114], especially if the audience was the common people. It would probably be presumptuous of me to compare the people of Europe in the late Middle Ages (12th to 14th centuries) with Mexican society, not of 1968 but of 1990. However, the effect it had on this same society seems to have been the

---

[113] At times it seems as if a new element (an exposed massacre) has been introduced into a traditional Mexican genre (the telenovela). This leads us to think that: 1) either the actors could not break away from the Great Popular Genre; or 2) it was necessary for it to happen this way, so that the middle and lower-middle class of Mexico could receive it without major difficulties.

[114] See the famous work by the Dutch writer, *The Waning of the Middle Ages* (I quote from memory), by Johan Huizinga (1920).

expected one. There was no great social or ethical change after *Rojo Amanecer,* but thousands of Mexicans were moved by the story.

We will not delve into a political or sociological analysis of the massacre. It is enough to add that it is presented as a "punitive lesson," of the same kind that the grandfather (a former–captain) demanded as a "deterrent" method and, obviously, as the ultimate expression of institutional sadism, of "state terrorism,"—although these last two concepts are not explicitly reflected in the film.

Psychological Typology of the Characters

Meanwhile, what happens with the characters? Here, too, it is very predictable (though this should not be read as false or demagogic characterizations).

The old man who coughs and gets up. He is the grandfather, he is the first, he is the lame military man. He doesn't need to tell us later that in his career he had risen to the rank of Captain. From the beginning, we intuit this through details that are too direct, like the shirt he insistently wears. It's not a military shirt, but it pretends to be one.

Daily life is besieged by contingency; however, even so, the events are *significant*. Even more so in a film, where symbols are usually accentuated. *In a work of art, we never expect things to be there by chance*, and even less so the clothing of the characters in a film. There are other "details" that

148

confirm the suspicion: the old man, the grandfather, asks his grandson to repeat military gestures.[115] Or the fondness for the game of tin soldiers, which the old man instills in his grandson.

The psychological types are very well-defined and even "stereotyped," though not to the extreme. Continuing with the military grandfather, his vision of the world and society is exactly what the viewer assumes:

"I can do it alone; I'm not useless," he replies to his daughter when she wants to help him pour his coffee. Immediately, he adds, "... unlike your children."

Soon, we not only have the profile of the typical grumpy old man, but we also know that his grandchildren, the "useless ones," think very differently. Ergo, we can already count them, in some way, among the victims. Not only of the events of Tlatelolco, but of a conservative and militarized society, summarized in the figure of the grandfather.

"Youth was different before," says the grandfather, and I'm almost ashamed to repeat it.

But there's more: when the family gathers for breakfast and the granddaughter turns on the *Beatles* on the radio, we immediately begin to fear the grandfather's phrase, which inevitably comes:

Grandfather: "They scream like faggots, not like men!"

---

[115] "Attention! At ease!" is one of the games played by the grandfather and grandson.

Mother: "Leave the kids alone. It's the fashion."

The grandfather detests those who wear long hair[116], and one of the "rebel-grandchildren" reminds him that Napoleon also had long hair.[117] This should doubly annoy the grandfather, since Napoleon is recognized not only for his victories (not so much for his defeats), but above all because he was a military man, a strategic genius. And we all know that there are no homosexuals in the army.[118]

The army is the grandfather's nostalgia, the "order."[119] When the shooting begins in the square, he will flash a secret smile. The grandfather participated in the revolution that established the current order. He has ideological reasons to be conservative and reactionary. But he also has personal, psychological reasons to demonstrate his confidence in the order that the military (that collective alter ego of the

---

[116] It is 1968, at the height of the hippie movement, of "cross-dressing" or the revolution we might call "Androgynous."

[117] When, in a much later scene, the "obedient grandson" confirms the accuracy of this comment in a history book, the grandfather will make an exception to the rule: "He wasn't [a faggot]."

118 In fact, parents often send their children there "to make them men," even if they have to endure humiliation, injustice, and violations (physical and moral).

[119] "Order" is a particularity of disorder, according to the physical theory of Chaos, just as the meaningful arrangement of a deck of cards —*1, 2, 3... n+1*— is a particularity among millions of other combinations we call "disordered" or "random." If we start from an ordered state (the world with its physical laws), *any other movement will lead to greater entropy*, that is, to greater disorder of matter, to the progressive aging of the Universe. Which, from an ethical and social point of view, we could translate as: *my order is the disorder of the other.*

grandfather) will restore, in that order that could annihilate his own family.

Grandfather: "There are many soldiers outside, snipers on the roof: [with professional pride] they are preparing a pincer movement. They've got the troublemakers occupied."[120]

Mother: "You were a soldier."

Grandfather: "It depends on what the kids do. They're going to give them a good scare. But don't worry. If it gets tough, they'll give them a good beating and throw them in jail."

Mother: "Maybe my children are out there!"

Grandfather: "Let them give them a scare. A few days locked up won't hurt them. Then their father will get them out. He has influence."

Mother: "Don't talk like that!"

Grandfather: "Your kids talk about Revolution all day and you don't say anything. I actually fought in one."

Later, the grandfather tells the obedient grandson: "This watch was given to me by General Rodríguez forty years ago. Things don't last that long anymore."

But while the grandfather considers himself the only one with possible moral values, it's clear that he is now a man who receives more orders than he can give. He is a retired Captain, someone who once held power but no

---

[120] It is unclear whether these snipers belonged to the army or directly to the government.

longer does. He does not have it in front of his daughter, much less in front of his son-in-law. He even demands respect from his grandchildren toward his son-in-law. Why? Because "thanks to your father we eat, thanks to your father you go to school." In other words, and taken to the social sphere, thanks to the government we eat; thanks to the government they go to school. *Thanks to the oppressor we are alive.*

His son-in-law, "the father," is the current patriarch. But a patriarch with limited power. Possessor of "great bureaucratic influence" —which he flaunts and uses whenever he can, as a tool of domination or as a tool of "survival"—, in the end he will see all his authority shattered by the dark forces of the government, which enter his home to prove it to him.

His power over his own rebel children is also limited. He threatens:

Father: "I'm warning you: stop being troublemakers. You don't mess with the government."

And later:

Father: "Bunch of irresponsible idiots, little rabbits of the communists who only want to sabotage the Olympics!"

The father also had a youth of militant rebellion, and what happened? The government usurped power. The story of failure repeats itself, and the young rebel (the father) is absorbed by the system, transformed into a respectable and influential family man, *a key piece of continuity.*

As for the sons, Jorge and Sergio, they are the typical embodiment of the rebellious, dreamy, idealistic student. Particularly, in this case, the leftist idealist, the romantic who feels compelled to resist and act in an unjust society, guided by the morality of certain icons, like Che Guevara's.

Rebel Son I: "What fault is it of ours that your generation [the father's] messed everything up?"

The young idealist doesn't feel the weight of past defeat. Hopes are always renewed. The young idealist feels that the world is born with him and, therefore, has reasons to hope despite repeated generational failures.

Rebel Son II: "[Our struggle is for] them to release our comrades. No one backs down here. The whole country is proud of its youth."

Mother: "You should focus on studying."

In other words, you should focus on "learning," on "integrating," on "assimilating" into the "natural order."

The mother, another important figure in the film, also plays a classic role: the woman who takes care of practical matters, not just of the house but of life in general. She is the one who mediates between the antagonistic positions of the men. She is the one who tends to the wounded young man when her sons bring him into their home. She is the image of compassion and sanity. But also, at times, of ideological mediocrity.

The mother is the one who organizes survival in the end, while her sons, "the revolutionaries" who rebel against the grandfather and against the government—against

God—, nevertheless take a submissive attitude toward the mother. The students, the sons, and their unknown companions become obedient children. It's likely due to a psychological conversion, a re-dimensioning of their characters. Though it's also likely due to the vulnerable position of the students: they are all "refugees," vulnerable, prone to being denounced; they are at the mercy of the lady of the house.

In any case, these "real" possibilities —considering the immediacy of the narrative—, do not seem to be significant for a more exhaustive reading of *Rojo Amanecer*.

As for the youngest daughter, aside from her very poor acting, she represents a character of generational "transition."

The following dialogue sums her up:

Daughter: "[when the phone line is cut] When I grow up, I'm going to have two phones, a big house, lots of money, and many servants."

Mother: "Do you plan to marry a millionaire?"

Daughter: "No, I'm going to be a dentist or a psychologist."

Too simple, of course. Too stereotypical. Practically nothing to salvage. It's clear that the mother represents the "old guard," the submissive woman-mother, while the daughter is the new liberated woman. However, —and I don't think this is hermeneutics either—, the daughter also represents a continuity: the class struggle, the desire to dominate others ("servants"), everything opposite to the vindication of the idealist brothers and, undoubtedly, of the film itself.

This will even be confirmed by a contradiction that can be seen at the end. In a dialogue with an unknown "revolutionary," the modern daughter asks:

Daughter: "Were you scared down there?"

Student: "Yes."

Daughter: "Leave that to the men."

Something similar happens with Luis, the seriously wounded student. His sister has been killed, and at one point he says: "What story am I going to tell my dad? How am I going to face going back home?" This serves to emphasize the continuity of the previous order through violence, through a lesson-teaching punishment.

Historical Context

Rojo Amanecer is set in a very specific historical moment, as we already know. But distracted viewers need not worry: at all times they will see a calendar announcing the precise date, many clocks carefully measuring the most dramatic moments, they will hear on the radio and television the news reports that will refer to the same event, although, of course, from the perspective of the manipulative Government.[121] If they don't know the date, it doesn't matter:

---

[121] At all times, and from the beginning, the radio refers to numbers of terrorists who were detained somewhere, who were planning to

one of the protagonists, almost at the beginning, will tear off a huge calendar page that says "Tuesday, October 1st" to clear up any doubt: it is

August 2, 1968.

As for the time, there's no problem: there will be clocks everywhere, indicating, with precision, when each shot was fired, when it began, and when it ended. And if anyone had doubts about the number of protesters who attended the *meeting* in Tlatelolco, the protagonist girl will tell them with historical accuracy: ten thousand people —though for that, a previous guessing game was necessary. How did the girl know? Well, that was also the younger brother's question: he probably counted them.

The repeated mention of *"only ten days left until the Olympic Games, Mexico '68"* not only serves to historically define the event that concerns us but also as a fact of the problem itself: the government intends to use the Games as a smokescreen for its population and, perhaps, for the rest of the world, and the "rebels" see it as an opportunity to draw attention or as a need to "pull back" the same propaganda curtain that the power has raised.

In a final scene (how predictable, how crude, my God!), all the protagonists gather around the television to listen to the news, like someone who has been in a street accident

---

endanger the Peace and Security of Mexico and other countries like Colombia, Uruguay, etc.)

and wants to see themselves confirmed in the "hyper-reality" of the Great Medium:

Television: "...*twenty people died as a result of a shootout provoked by two groups of students* [Etc.] *Mexico* is a country where freedom prevails [...] Only ten days remain until the start of the Mexico '68 Olympics."

A discourse to which, with insults and tearful demonstrations of rage, the students respond by spreading the new official version, the one that will only come to light after many years[122].

Everything is historically true, or at least it is the truth we share today almost unanimously. It is the truth of the silenced (almost useless, because, as always, it is heard when compassion no longer reaches the protagonists, the victims, when it no longer serves them and, therefore, confirms once again that *when justice is delayed, it does not arrive.*[123]

Ethical Discourse

But if the viewer doesn't know what kind of government Mexico had in 1968, it doesn't matter: it's clear from the start who the good guys and the bad guys are. In fact, I think even an ultra-conservative viewer might risk

---

[122] We are referring to the massacre itself. Not even the 1998 commission could find those responsible.

[123] And I say "almost useless," because human injustice knows no bounds and, therefore, it is always good to preserve Memory.

sympathizing with Che Guevara, not because of what they might know about him, but in solidarity with the students murdered and tortured by the arrogance of power, which will be revealed in its rawest, most realistic, and most credible state when, in one of the final scenes, a small group of armed men enter the house-stage and threaten the entire family with their weapons. Even the powerful "influence" of the father, who apparently wields it from his bureaucratic position, is of no use:

Man I: "So you're very influential? [Then, showing his weapon] *This* is more influential, you bastard!"

It becomes clear, then, —as it became clear to the rest of us Latin Americans, —that if reason doesn't matter to justify despotic power, even less do the most basic moral principles, noted since the times of Moses and the *Bhagavad-Gita*, and translated 3,400 years later into the Universal Declaration of Human Rights.

Even worse, in my opinion, are the descriptions of the young victims.

More fitting for a testimonial documentary, where the goal is to elicit tears from the witness, than for a film that could raise ethical questions about an event of great significance for Mexican society —and for the world.

On the other hand, and considering the Mexican audience of 1989, the character of the grandfather ends up prioritizing the value of family over that of the army. He tries to protect them using what little remains of his status as a captain and his shattered pride. The grandfather opts for

158

what remains of his humanity and seeks to protect his rebel grandchildren, his family. But he fails in the face of the barbarism he himself helped impose in the past and defended until just a few hours earlier.

In other words, *the ethical version of the reactionary is defeated* by the injustice of those he previously supported.

As for the scenes following the massacre, I think they suffer from overacting, as we noted earlier, on the part of the actors, and from melodrama on the part of the screenwriter.

And, as if all that weren't enough, a dramatic ending in the worst style. The bad guys kill the good guys, with great arbitrariness and showing all the blood. When almost no characters are left alive, —the only thing it has in common with a Shakespearean tragedy—is that the obedient grandson walks over the corpses of his family; then he continues down the stairs over other unknown corpses. A kind of Future Avenger or Future Consciousness seems to promise us justice from the shadows of time (to be realized by the generation of young adults in 1989). All seasoned with an implausible performance by the child... But it's not his fault.

Justification

At times, great works of art have been made from small, seemingly insignificant themes. At other times, the opposite results have been achieved: small works on great themes. I think this is the case with *Rojo Amanecer*.

However, the film has a value that we should not underestimate. Made with limited financial resources and, —above all, —in a context of taboos and officialist discourses, *Rojo Amanecer* manages to bring to the public stage, not without courage, an event silenced by power and which will remain, for a long time, an open wound in Mexican society. It does so in a melodramatic and overacted manner, with the pretense of containing its own interpretation, agreed, but its mission is perhaps that of the cursed cartoonist who points out the sore spot. And it's well done.

Its production and release were in 1989. It would take nine years for an official investigative commission to be established in 1998, which, in the end, would not mean much more than what [124]Rojo Amanecer *meant.*

Rojo Amanecer may be an insignificant film in the history of Latin American cinema, but it is significant for the society from which and for which it was made. In this sense, it would not only have achieved its own objective but would also be entirely justified.

A Reading Through Mas'ud Zavarzaeh

Rojo Amanecer is not a political pamphlet. It has documentary pretensions but, above all, there is a clear need for

---

124 Like all "investigative commissions," promoted by Latin American political power: sooner or later, they become "justifying commissions" for the crimes of each day.

"denunciation" and "vindication." That is, in other words, a need for an *ethical judgment*.

The facts are not nuanced by doubt. Nor is the ideological or political context exposed or discussed. *The urgency of vindication does not allow it*. It is a reinterpretation of the past, as M. Zaverzadeh might say, "required by the ideological needs of the present"[125]

The same Zavarzaeh, when analyzing the tradition in American cinema, warns that tradition is a way of "resolving" the ideological contradictions of capitalist society, its positive valuation of change (of the new) and of stability —the permanence of power, fear of the new126— at the same time. "Tradition —says M.Z.— in other words, dehistoricizes history and produces a timeless instance in which things change without ever becoming different"127

In this sense, and in line with what we pointed out earlier, we could say that *Rojo Amanecer* "dehistoricizes history," presenting a past event, loaded with historical, social, economic, and political significance, to focus it on a single point: the "permanent" values of compassion, tolerance,

---

[125] As a result of [an] homogenization of the past [...] history is a free-floating moment that is not the effect of economic, political, legal, and philosophical practices of a society but a moral fable —an interpretation of the past as is required by the ideological needs of the present. Mas'ud Zavarzaeh, Seeing films politically, pg. 154-155.
[126] The resistance to change, the rejection of the new, represented, in Rojo amanecer, by the family of the young rebels.
[127] Op. Cit. Pg. 155.

and Human Rights —the denunciation of injustice, of the barbarism of state power.

However, and unlike what M. Z. noted regarding American cinema, *Rojo Amanecer* seeks to oppose the prevailing ideology, both the current one and that of the time —regardless of whether it succeeds or not, regardless of whether it ends up, through a paradoxical mechanism, serving the ideology of the time, as a necessary catharsis that will relieve tension and allow the continuity of the dominant class and ideology.

In his analysis of *Lost in America*, M. Z. warns that the behavior of those who have placed themselves on the margins of a social order they question —Linda, Davis, and the hippies— confirms, by itself, the dominant ideology.

> [...] The two hippies decide to privatize the contestation of values [and] make their separate peace with the world. [They] are in a sense not really critical of the specificity of their own political situation. Instead of seeking a concrete history of oppositional citizens contesting the practices of capitalist regime, they have traditionalized the conventional life-style of the "bohemian" margin. They emulate mere "dissent" and even then traditionalize (de-historicized).[128]
>
> [...] In their traditionalization of the (bohemian) past, they are as much involved in nostalgia.[129]

---

[128] Op. Cit. Pg. 162
[129] Op. Cit. Pg. 163

We could draw a quick parallel with the rebellious youth of *Rojo Amanecer*, with some variations: the rebellious students do not "privatize" their resistance but, on the contrary, "socialize" it. Of course, sooner or later they will end up justifying not only the permanence in power of the dominant classes but also the violence and the famous "states of exception."

However, we must not overlook that all these observations, those of M. Z. and those we could apply to Tlatelolco, are observations, first and foremost, about the logic of ideological domination in which societies, particularly capitalist society, are structured.

Now, what role would films like *Rojo Amanecer* play in this logic? From this perspective, the answer does not seem obvious. In fact, the results could be disparate and inverse. *Rojo Amanecer* could be the vehicle for that "traditionalization" of marginality, of resistance —resigned atemporality, an immanent element of social "discomfort," of the same category as drug addicts—; or, on the contrary, it could simply mean a legitimization of disobedience.

Both are extremes of the same spectrum. In between lie more plausible nuances. Probably Zavarzaeh himself has already synthesized it as follows:

"People may 'dissent[130]', but dissent, it is implied, is really a form of adolescent political tantrums: one grows up and recovers from it or one regresses into life-long infantilism and is thus banished from the society of adults. [Dissent] is ineffective because it is an idealistic distancing from the existing institutions of capitalism and not a materialist critique of its operations nor an intervention in its economic order and class organizations of culture."[131]

Neither in *Rojo Amanecer* nor in *Lost in America* do the protagonists succeed in their "rebellious" choice. The North American film has a somewhat happy, humorous ending (especially since B-movies all end with a joke and a smile). This is not the case with *Rojo Amanecer*, where blood and defeat abound.

In both, skepticism prevails:

An adult person cannot step out of the dominant practice of the culture.[132]

---

[130] The difference between "dissent" and "disobedience" is important. It is one of the main characteristics of the future society of the present century.
[131] Op. Cit, Pg. 165
[132] Op. Cit. Pg. 168.

LA VENDEDORA DE ROSAS

Gaviria, 1998

The naturalist novel emerged in Europe in a context of misery among the new urban classes, a product of the Industrial Revolution, that is, of Progress. Films like *La vendedora de rosas* belong to a genre that, more than naturalist, aims to be hyperrealist. For some reason, neither naturalism nor hyperrealism emerge and develop in the upper classes—perhaps because there we will never find anything natural and even less something "real," something that has not been falsified by sophistication and power.

This type of artistic expression is inseparable from the social drama in which it is not only "produced" but also reflected. It is the tragic version of postmodern *reality shows*; it is the least false version of reality.

At first glance, *La vendedora de rosas* presents itself as a denunciation with the emphasis on the vulnerable and tragic situation of street children. And before that, of girls, these multiply vulnerable—and violated—subjects of our societies. Probably that has also been the intention of its creators. But I believe its gravitation encompasses much more.

La vendedora de rosas is not a film in the Hollywood sense of the word: it is a painting, an overwhelming mural. Extending the comparison with classical canons, we could say that it does not even have a plot, and if it tells a story, it does so in the same terms as a photograph, a brief series of photographs, a brief image on the TV news. In fact, the dialogues are not understood, or are barely understood. Because the words come from the mouth of a drug addict, a drunk, or because, in fact, they say nothing and are limited to a small number of words, the few that these victim-perpetrators learned to insult—"gonorrhea" serves for everything—to say little more than what they can express with gestures, with silences, with a stick, with a knife, with a gun in hand, with a man's hand on the buttocks of a girl who is no longer surprised, who no longer has room for new traumas because she has almost ceased to be a person.

La vendedora de rosas is an image that screams, not with the logical neatness of a detective novel, but through the overwhelming repetition of a real drama that is also repeated. Repeated to death—real—of its protagonists. A fleeting moment in the brief lives of these girls and not so fleeting in the life of Latin American societies. Especially in recent years.

Poverty has always existed—I don't know if "dignified poverty" ever existed or if this type of dignity was only an invention of the dominant classes—, but what is perhaps new is the volume, intensity, and violence of the eternal dance that life has maintained—at times in an obscene way—with death. I believe a single image encapsulates *La vendedora de rosas* and, by extension, the reality of that region of the world: the face of a child speaking with a glue

166

bottle at their nose. All the remaining violence is implied, because if the filmmakers of this movie intervened in anything, it was not only in showing what is hidden but in not showing what is accepted, in sparing us—us, educated and overwhelmed viewers—the violence of more reality. Because it's already enough to bother us with the glue; it wasn't necessary to put us in the uncomfortable situation of witnessing more tears, explicit sexual violations.

Of course, if we set aside what matters most, we can analyze the artistic result a bit. The mere choice of a few elements—no matter how representative they may be—from a vast, almost infinite or at least unmanageable set, results in a judgment, both ethical and aesthetic. Among these choices is the date, which is highly symbolic. In fact, I don't believe there is a more symbolic and connotation-filled date in our world than Christmas. Not just for Christians. This choice not only allows for the addition of a new element in the series—drugs, fantasy, lights, gunpowder—: the fleetingness of illusion, of fireworks. As we've seen in other examples, religion also appears here as a problem but, above all, the Church, directly or indirectly, as a symbol of the contradictions of our societies, as a reference for hope and futility, for theological mystery—why does pain, does Evil exist, if God is Almighty?— and for institutional farce.

For the protagonist, the virgin and the mother are the same thing[133]. Both represent a promise of liberation. The virgin promises a *future liberation*; the mother promises to rescue her *from the past*. Here the present contrasts violently and points us to the science-fiction-catastrophe genre, where the world has succumbed to chaos and people—a submerged class, far from the powerful, as always—desperately seek to survive amidst the worst misery and abandonment, amidst violence and alienation. *La vendedora de rosas* tells us that this future has already arrived, that the chaos is now, that the world has already been lost. Destruction, decay—moral and material—coexist with elements of modernity[134]. Except here, unlike in Hollywood, there are no promises of redemption, no heroes organizing resistance, incubating rebellion. There is no hope, only death. Death to achieve virginal liberation; death—as indeed happens—to return to the arms of the mother.

From a symbolic point of view, it is no coincidence that the mother, along with her entire family, appears in Mónica's dreams and hallucinations as characters from the past, gathered around a table[135] —the true Christmas— and

---

[133] This is not only demonstrated by the mother's physical attitude but also by the protagonist's imaginary substitution of the statue of the Virgin Mary in a carnivalesque procession.

[134] Skates, telephones, watches, televisions, cars, motocross, firearms, fireworks.

[135] In a circle of drug addicts, one of the children offers the "dessert": more glue, which he distributes in streams to his companions.

warmly neat in their gestures and attire. At other times, and with other characters, this same background will be alluded to: *the dissolution of the family* as a cause or symptom of decay and the return to it as a possible path to redemption[136]. It is the lost paradise. And the most serious thing of all: It is the lost paradise. And the most serious thing of all: none of this is pure fiction.

Now, La vendedora de rosas not only bothers because of the repetition of a reality that shocks us, but—from a formal point of view—it bothers us because we cannot recognize in it the traditional model of narration. The absence of plot, the contingency of events, is omnipresent. "(…) *in order to counter the aesthetic of realism, which was hopelessly compromised with bourgeois ideology, as well as Hollywood cinema, avant grade and feminism filmmakers must take an oppositional stance against narrative "illusionism" and in favor of formalism. The assumption was that "foregrounding the process itself, privileging the signifier, necessarily disrupts aesthetics unity and forces the spectator's attention on the means of production of meaning.*"[137]

---

[136] I am referring to the girl's return home, the appearance of the father—in white pants—who rescues the dark-skinned girl, etc. When the father and his daughter leave, the other girls watch from a window of the boarding house, and one of them says: "With a dad like that, I'd leave too."

[137] Technologies of Gender, Aesthetic and feminist Theory.

TIEMPO DE REVANCHA

Adolfo Aristaran, Emilio Kauderer, *1981.*

The Word and Silence

Over the past twenty years, the main theme in Argentine cinema has been, without respite, the dark years of the past military dictatorship (1974-1983). In all cases, —social, political, ethical, and economic— criticism is a common factor. I believe that if Latin American cinema differs from Hollywood cinema, it is not so much because of its resources but because of its marginal discourse, a certain tradition of resistance to the dominant ideology. On the other hand, in Latin America, it is almost impossible to conceive of art for art's sake, as a formal game of sensory effects, perhaps because we never had a belle époque: in our art —and particularly in cinema—, ethics and aesthetics form an indivisible body, but also a permanent concern, a lucid awareness of discontent.

This also shows us two things: a period of political democracy and, at the same time, of social injustice. Let us think, then, of a time (1981) and a place (Argentina) where not even the formality of democracy or the harmless right to dissent existed. As has happened before, and as it happens today in other countries in similar situations, the only way out is metaphor, the Trojan horse.

Time for Revenge is both. Produced and released when the military dictatorship was beginning to falter, this film starring Federico Luppi does not directly confront the government of the time. However, its criticism is directed at class power —the primary beneficiary of the military dictatorship—. In this sense, it has an ideological background rooted in Marxism and early Christianity.

From the very beginning, we see the different symbols of a Christmas that in every way resembles New York, the paradigm of the corporate and financial city. The image of Santa Claus (a religious icon of Marlboro and Coca-Cola), the background choir, and a man who, with a businesslike gesture, approaches a tall, pristine office tower that could well be located, along with the others surrounding it, somewhere in Manhattan.

But we are in Buenos Aires. Here, in the first dialogue, in the first interior scene, we become aware of an obscene transmigration: a former union leader seeks to erase his past to secure a position in a copper mine. That is, here we have a representative of the margin absorbed, in the classic style, by the center. Of course, that center has relied on despotic political power, but it continues to act according to its best strategies: the persuasion of the correct discourse, the ethics of "free competition," of individual and national progress.

Bursaco, the mega-corporation, is the religion that must legitimize every action and every discourse. In the interview of the prospective employee with the manager, the latter repeatedly asks: "Do you like your job, Bengoa?" It is a test of faith, an initiation of the aspirant into the sect. We know that not just anyone enters that kind of brotherhood —a small job in a Big Corporation—, and for that, an initiatory transformation is always necessary. At the same time, the Manager insists on clarifying that everything exists thanks to a single man (god, let's write it in lowercase). Every mega-corporation is a hierarchical religion, like the Church, with a god, a pope, with its saints and ministers, with a single ethic and a single faith. One must be with it or be its enemy; one must respect and love it without concessions, even if in its defense one of its "faithful" must lose their life in some useless explosion. To ensure that the candidate has been ethically integrated into the center, the manager will not only seek to ensure that he does not have an unfaithful past —of a rebellious unionist; no converted pigs are accepted— but also that he possesses the greatest virtue a man aspiring to identify with the Bursaco religion can have: the candidate's ambition. To demonstrate this, the former rebel says, with an innocent face and the calm of a mercenary: "Bursaco pays, I work. The rest is not my problem." A moment in which, at least in appearance, the initiate demonstrates possessing the ethical values necessary to be part of the company and, as a consequence, to survive as a man and as a citizen.

However, as events unfold, the hidden past resurfaces, and with it, the awareness of a defeated ethics, not only by power but, above all, by its own concession to it.

Now, how has Bengoa (the protagonist, the one who "comes to") achieved this provisional transformation? With

173

the same weapons as the enemy: he has simulated, he has lied, he has brought out his ambitious, unscrupulous side —his amoral side— to achieve a personal goal. He has learned the ethics of anti-ethics, or it has always been a constitutive part of his persona.

"I took the risk and they sent me to the front —he says later, justifying himself through his Christian-unionist past— and they sent me to the front. And what did I gain?"

However, this transformation of personality in a man already graying cannot be sustained for long. And this premonition already appears as a warning from his father: "One day they will provoke you, and you will open your mouth," which also constitutes a symbolic key to the film: *opening one's mouth to raise a voice of protest has until now brought more injustice, repression, and defeat.* The margin cannot use the same strategies as the center, because the center does it better, its voice is stronger, and, worse still, it is more credible, more "centered," more "realistic," and "mature."

As soon as they arrive in the mining region, a subtle event occurs: Bengoa carries his own luggage, while the engineer tells him not to, that "El Golo" (the Indian) is there for that. Bengoa does not accept, and the engineer gives him a distrustful look. The new convert demonstrates dangerous behavioral values; his consciousness as dominated-dominator is not clear.

But the past returns. Among his subordinates, he will find an old comrade from his unionist militancy, who has also been integrated into the center.

174

"I'm an angel," says the old friend. "I don't protest. You have to eat. I play along. *Don't speak*, don't protest. This is hell."

At the same time, Bengoa's wife suggests he distance himself from his friend: "We came here to live in peace," she tells him.

Finally, the main motive of the plot is revealed: the simulation of an accident by Bengoa and Bruno with the aim of collecting a significant compensation, as a result of a workplace accident that should leave Bruno mute. To do this, both former unionists plan to use the same weapons as the enemy, legitimized by the ethics of the center, that is, personal gain. And if the attack is against those who remain unlegitimized for two defeated rebels, all the better.

But things do not turn out as planned. Bruno chickens out and, in his last-minute attempt to flee, dies in the explosion. Bengoa takes his place accidentally and, upon being rescued, pretends he cannot speak.

Up to this point, Bengoa will position himself from the ethics of the victor to claim the compensation, not as a result of a legal trial but through a negotiation-blackmail that a complicit and unscrupulous lawyer will carry out. However, when Bengoa and his lawyer visit the house of the "one man," the owner of the business empire, with the aim of negotiating the blackmail, the great turning point in the character's life and in the discourse of the film itself occurs. Upon learning that the deaths of his comrades were due to the exploitation of a copper mine that had no copper, Bengoa rejects the offer from the owner of Bursaco, which had far exceeded the initial ambitions of his lawyer and himself.

It is at this moment that the main discursive merit of *Time for Revenge* which is, at the same time, an ethical and ideological discovery —if not strategic, as well—, is masterfully represented with an apparently common metaphor. Bengoa decides to go to trial and thus embark on his greatest battle against the Empire. Larsen, the mercenary lawyer, tells him that "the best way to screw them is by taking their money." However, Bengoa understands the opposite: the loss of money, like the gain, are part of the rules of the capitalist game. They are not, however, accepting new rules from a marginal individual who has decided not to sell out. He does not so much pursue the destruction of Bursaco, the revelation of its immorality and vulnerability —which would be an almost impossible task, much more so for a single man—, but his own ethical vindication and his revenge.

It could be understood —and I believe the authorities of the time must have done so, since if there was one thing they lacked, it was insight—, that in the end, "institutionalized justice" triumphs. However, this is a mistake: Bengoa *uses* that justice which, in a way, is Bursaco's support. Bengoa wins the trial by lying, though he does not use a single word. The lie and the dishonor of formal justice is another of the secret inhabitants of the Trojan horse.

From that moment on, everything depends on him. Everything depends on his ability to *not utter a single word*. Ultimately, he succeeds in his goal, but with a paradoxical exception. His past as a union activist represents the one who denounces, *the one who promotes the use of speech*. But speech is colonized by the discourse of the dominant ideology, and thus, it not only fails to destroy the relationship of domination and dependence on the center, but above all, it becomes —the word of the dissident—, yet another reason that legitimizes the unrestrained oppression of central power. Even one of the characters —El Golo, the descendant of the Indians who fought for their land and paid for their defeat with death or exile—, agrees to testify in the trial. *He speaks*, and for that, they kill him.

Time for Revenge culminates with a scene that is more symbolic than plausible, but necessary: the protagonist triumphs and utters a single word in the shower, in a private space: "we won." But after realizing that the enemy remains threatening —it has been offended but not destroyed—, he cuts out his tongue with the cold precision of a surgeon. His tongue did not serve to save him but, on the contrary, ultimately subjected and enslaved him. To make matters worse, his integration into the orbit of the ideological center was thanks to his tongue. With it, he had lied and concealed his past. He had not needed it to defeat the power, to vindicate himself as an ethical man, to honor his memory and justify his own existence, but through it, he could fall again. As his father had said at the beginning, one day he would say what he shouldn't and would be lost once more.

Now, should we take this discovery literally or as a metaphor? I lean toward the second possibility. It is not only understood as Mahatma Gandhi understood it, as a form of passive resistance, but as a dialectical strategy: a relationship of domination is not overcome by using the same weapons as the oppressor nor by opposing him from an antagonistic position. The dominant ideology is, at its core, a dialectical relationship maintained mutually by the oppressor and the oppressed. The rupture of this relationship, the non-recognition of its language, is what threatens the oppressor's power.

Time for Revenge is structured like a classic police procedural film. There are no technical innovations or major formal experiments. It does not demand our constant interpretive attention; at times —especially at the end— we must simply resign ourselves to sensing the tension typical of the police genre and wait for the trial and events to be resolved. There is also no excessive work on the symbolic elements characteristic of Latin American cinema. The costumes hardly matter, the final settings, colors, or spaces hardly matter. The behaviors become plain, they do not require a hermeneutic or psychoanalytic effort; they are not more real but more realistic.

Nevertheless, we should not include it in the vast group composed of the reasonable, vulgar, and classic game of the Anglo-Saxon genre. Like so many other works of Latin American cinema, its epic lies in viewing its own society from the margins. Its flaws are often the critique, the questioning, and the market's incomprehension. Its greatest virtue, perhaps, is having achieved a magnificent metaphor for the dialectic of power, a harsh and acidic irony of the class struggle.

DIARIOS DE MOTOCICLETA

Walter Salles, 2004

In 1773, the false "pure Indian," Concolorcorvo, traveled across South America with Don Alonso, starting from the Río de la Plata and ending in Peru. Not only is the geographic route similar to the one undertaken nearly two centuries later by Ernesto Guevara and Alberto Granados, but also the intended intellectual legitimization of the chronicle and the rejection of the bookish historization of Europe. In his travel diary, Concolorcorvo noted that the Creoles knew more about European history than their own, a topic that reappears in The Motorcycle Diaries in the same mythical space: Peru. But if the ideology of the false Inca victimized the selfless conquerors and defamed the savage inhabitants of these lands, the perspective of the new Latin American martyr had to be the opposite. As Joseph Campbell tells us (in *The Hero with a Thousand Faces*), the mythical hero must make an initiation journey, descend into hell before enlightenment. In the Latin American language of liberation (Paulo Freire), this means *concientização*. Once achieved, the communication of the New Man follows, and finally his sacrifice. The myth is more than reality and less as well. Mircea Eliade (in *The Myth of the Eternal Return*) reminds us of its oral nature, that is, removed from the complexities of written text and linear historical time. Every myth, once its archetype is reached, remains unchanged, functional to a certain knowledge that is assumed to be inherent in every human being, beyond their time and context.

In *The Motorcycle Diaries*, the filmic text itself includes, at the beginning, a self-reference to another famous and unequal pair (necessarily *unequal*, I understand, because they are, moreover, dialectical heroes): Don Quixote and Sancho Panza. The identification of *La Poderosa* with Rocinante —both paradoxical names— aims to complete the mythical-aesthetic composition; the motorcycle fulfills a symbolic function, to the point of fetishism, as it quickly disappears in the story but dominates the title and all the iconography of the work. The Granados-Guevara duo will reverse their roles as the narrative progresses, just as Cervantes' characters did in their time. But this last reference is lost in the film. It is more important to note that the allusion to the Manchego antihero is also a direct —though not deliberate— reference to the *Latin hero*, since Cervantes: the hero in the times of the Counter-Reformation—just like Robin Hood in the times of the Black Death, peasant revolts, and the questioning of the Papacy—ventures into the world, into adventure, to seek justice. As if it were a dark gnostic heritage, for our Catholic subculture the world is the order of the demiurge, of evil. Latin America is one of its latest creations. Therefore, like El Zorro, the Latin hero can only be marginal. Different—and not without historical paradox—for the Protestant hero (Superman

180

& Co., including a neogothic hero like Batman), the good are in power and the evil are hidden in the underground, in deep caves, threatening to take over a world that already has an owner. Unlike another unequal pair, Holmes-Watson, Superman is not a dialectical hero and thus is solitary; when Batman loses Robin in the '90s, he radicalizes that same profile: pure expression of brute force, of hegemony that neither questions itself nor gives account of its actions. "Fighting for justice" is nothing more than restoring the prevailing hegemonic power that the marginalized seek to destroy. Both, the Latin hero and the Anglo-Saxon hero, conceal their identities; the former hide from the central power, the latter from the marginal villains. Both cross-dress, because power, like truth—since Heraclitus—is always hidden. But if the Latin hero is mythical, the Anglo-Saxon is a mythomaniac. The transcendent battle (for power, for truth) takes place in heaven or hell, but never in the middle plane of mortals. *The Motorcycle Diaries* narrates the birth of one of these mythical heroes (of Latin profile) who, in the course of their long journey, must descend into Hades before ascending to Olympus. The irresistible attraction lies in narrating it from the human, vulnerable, non-mythical space. Similar would be a film that narrates the life of Jesus before his baptism in the Jordan River.

Since the independence of Latin America never truly happened, the emergence of a redemptive figure was natural, and it is natural for their mythical survival. Deeper than the ideology they embodied as the supreme ideal was the need for a messiah who would rescue a people long oppressed, stuck, like few others, in their own past, under the double temptation of killing the oppressor or letting themselves be seduced by him to the limits of "carnal relations" (sic Carlos Menem). Now, although the historical Che Guevara is much more than an archetype, it is only this, the mythical archetype, that appears in the subtext of *The Motorcycle Diaries*—and in the consumers of Anglo-Saxon "rebels"—recreated from their own human weaknesses. Despite everything, the myth of Che Guevara cannot reach the absolute status of ancient myths. It is prevented by the vast amount of written documents and a modern mindset inclined towards critical doubt. On the other hand, it is facilitated by an ultramodern culture: having renounced its primary vocation, revolution, our time has opted for iconolatry and the mythologization of history, for a thought based on languages—on independent systems of games, like the computational—rather than on ideas that seek a global understanding of each of their parts. Immersed in a sea of digital texts, the ultramodern mind rests on the micro narratives of advertising, on symbolic images, and on slogans, which are simplifying and repetitive. The new fetish bears the mark of its own time: aesthetic consumption and anti-dialectical advertising. For the latter, beyond any narrative lies the direct, fragmentary message. There is no relationship between one event and the next, which is not understood as a flaw but as a virtue. (This is our era of social and historical autism, typical of a transition.) But for each

182

event to enter the circle of consumption, it must conform to de-problematizing parameters. Art abandons its aspirations of changing consumers' expectations and specializes in satisfying those very expectations, according to a hegemonic culture characterized by its mythomaniac practice. That is, the work of art—in this case *The Motorcycle Diaries*—must distance itself from the "politically incorrect," which also includes confirming a profile of rebellion, of the hero's individuality. Thus, the paradigm of the integrated rebel of our time is forged, for whom rebellion consists of changing hair color and piercing tongues to "express themselves." Similarly, the hero or apocalyptic intellectual becomes a lubricant for the great machinery, a complacent official of the masses.

Both the shortcomings and virtues of the modern myth affect the film *The Motorcycle Diaries*: if there is no absolute myth, but a problematic myth, then no reconstruction of the traditional myth can be safe from the extremes of criticism. Every work of art has a political component and at the same time is more than politics; but sometimes this dimension is so weighty that it becomes as artificial to exclude it from an analysis of the work as it is to describe the smile of the Mona Lisa without considering some kind of emotion in the reference. To this we add that, as is the case with almost all post-Revolution Cuban cinema, the most important text is not explicit in the work itself, in the film narrative, but in its own context. That is, it is what we might call a *historical work of art*. Unlike *Oedipus Rex* (a

183

mythological work of art), for which the context is irrelevant or barely anecdotal. Excluding the political-historical context in films of the New Latin American Cinema and in the more recent Cuban cinema (both on and off the island) would be an exaggeration akin to reducing Donald Duck to its ideological subtext. Which is not impossible, because the subtext exists, but the result of such an exercise is more akin to art itself than to critical analysis: it is a free creation, stimulated by the reference; not a critical creation, conditioned by it. The Hollywood context, on the other hand, can be disregarded, not because of its absence but because of its omnipresence. Revolutionary or problematic cinema is a response to a hegemony and thus becomes political art. Similarly, heterosexuality, being assumed as hegemonic, loses its (explicit) political character; the gay, on the other hand, by inevitably confronting reclamation, transforms their sexuality into a political fact.

In *The Motorcycle Diaries* the hybridity consists of uniting these two poles, in unequal parts. The revolutionary hero, once the historical threat has passed, does not become a museum piece but something more harmless: they are integrated. But for their digestion to occur, they must first be pasteurized until they achieve a character opposite to that of the historical Che Guevara. The myth also loses its sharp edges (political, for example); it becomes a product of consumption: fast, easy, disposable. If ostensibly the ethics of the rebel prevail, ultimately their neutralization as a problematic element triumphs, as there is no material commitment from the neo-rebel but rather their own symbolic complacency. The ethics of the rebel are neutralized by the hegemonic aesthetics.

On another level, I understand that it is not the emotionality of the film, as critics have abundantly noted, its weakest point. After Bertolt Brecht, it seems almost impossible to recognize any merit in cathartic art. After the great Nietzsche and the not-so-great Ortega y Gasset, the masses have become the recipients of all the disdain of the cultured intellect. Market and spirit are antagonistic, just as quantity is to quality; therefore, according to this school, the people and depth must also be opposed. But art is nothing without emotions, and these are not the property of an elite of intellectuals (let alone unshakable intellectuals). On the other hand, for this kind of complex, rejection is easier than apology, since in the former the critic places themselves on a higher plane than the work in question, while in the latter they relinquish that privilege. Criticism has mocked the "sentimentalism" of *The Motorcycle Diaries*, which is typical of any commentator who positions themselves in a privileged plane simply by virtue of their smirk: crying, being moved, is for inferior beings, generally feminine and with little critical insight. Just to be safe, one must mock the emotions. But if this film manages to move the audience, it is by its own merit, especially when it does so in moments of certain kitsch. Now, if this innocence is the reason for the emotion of a social group, we should recognize that our judgment must be relative to the objectives of

185

a work of art. Shakespeare also makes us cry with a cheesy and romantic love like that of Romeo and Juliet. (Today, other geniuses make us cry with more sophisticated loves; but it is more of a critical weeping.)

We can note, then, that the greatest flaws of this film lie not in its ability to move a social group x, but in its inability to sustain the emotion in a social group y—assumed to be superior to social group x—, interrupting it with moments of implausible innocence on the part of the protagonist. From this perspective (y), *The Motorcycle Diaries* fails at several points, progressively so until reaching an ending far below any expectation. If the story could not include the tragic moment of his death—which would have completed the classical canon for a social group x—at least it could have left the ending open with a genuine psychological change in the protagonist. A journey and a process of consciousness-raising deserve, at least, a bildungsroman.

However, *The Motorcycle Diaries* is sustained by an infinite metatext: without it, the film would be the *road movie* of an idle young bourgeois from middle-class Buenos Aires. Nothing in it shows us an exceptional man, quite the opposite. Even if, on one hand, it attempts to highlight the protagonist's original honesty, his intellectual faculties are constantly called into question. The "Latin Americanist" speech that captures the attention of Alberto and the others during his birthday party at the leprosarium in San Paulo is more characteristic of Cantinflas than of a future myth of global politics. The ending is totally disappointing. The farewell between Ernesto and Alberto at an airport in Venezuela is pathetic. One must imagine a Che Guevara confessing, with great difficulty in oral expression, that the trip had changed him. Wasn't that, precisely, the point? But the protagonist must say it because the film fails to show that change. It was also unnecessary for him to comment, as if he didn't believe it himself: "So many injustices, right?..." followed by ellipses that reveal the absence of what was most abundant in the historical Che Guevara, in the dialectical hero: his loquacity, even if at times messy; his literary creativity condensed into aphorisms, later turned into popular sayings or even the catchphrases of Jean-Paul Sartre himself. If these words could have been the actual words spoken by Ernesto Guevara at that precise moment, they should have been removed for being implausible. In daily life, most of what we say is trivial and even stupid. But we try not to put it in a book. Much less at the end of a film that features Che Guevara as its central protagonist. All of which makes us think that when Salles chose the theme of his next film, he completed half of a great work; but the other half was too large.

Finally, we note that the song by Jorge Drexler, winner of the first Oscar for a Spanish-language song, does not form part of the emotionality of the narrative. This association, music-history, has historically been fruitful: when one of the pair's terms failed, it was saved by the other. In this case, the award-winning song was relegated to the end, as the musical curtain for the credits, when the hypnosis of the story has been interrupted and the audience begins to think about where they left their car. Drexler has compositions far more impactful than "On the Other Side of the River," but, like any award, this one is also part of a context that needs to be analyzed more broadly by critics. One of the keys is the very fact that the academy's mythomania did not allow him to perform his own song on the Big Night (the absence of a Che García Bernal at the award ceremony, in protest over this fact, is the response of the integrated rebel that aligns with market expectations and the style of his language), choosing Antonio Banderas (El Zorro), for his image and not, obviously, for his voice. It would have been equivalent to handing the Nobel Prize to Mario Benedetti on the condition that the acceptance speech be delivered by Jennifer Lopez, explaining how she planned to urgently redecorate the White House if she were president of the United States (sic).

RETRATO DE TERESA

Pastor Vega, 1979

The voice and silence beyond the explicit discourse

Pastor Vega returns, in *Portrait of Teresa*, to his old love: addressing a social issue through the individual drama of a woman. We could say that the central theme of this film is "the ideological oppression of women in a machista society." As a theme, it is almost a cliché. As a social problem, it is no less real or dramatic, which justifies a film. Probably in the '70s, the issue of gender was not a central social debate in Cuba nor in many other Latin American countries. Yes, it certainly was, in academic circles and among artists and intellectuals like those of the ICAIC group. Teresa's challenge to her husband at the end of the film ("if I had done the same thing, would it have been the same? Answer me") is not a problematization but a rhetorical question. It's no coincidence that he doesn't respond. As rhetorical as some observations by the other Teresa (de Laurentis) when she refers to the "sexuality" of Romance languages (better to say "languages"). Roman Jakobson uncovers (or exposes) the idea that there is no reason for a universal law in the reference to the Moon as feminine and the Sun as

masculine.138 As if the opposite possibility were something terrible, the origin of all the oppressions and unhap-
piness of women throughout history, de Laurentis cannot
hide her partisan—and not at all analytical—precondition
with the humorous and ironic expression "Thank heavens
for that!139 (4)

Now, if this is the justification (to address "the situation
of the ideological oppression of women in a machista,
anachronistic society"), it's clear that the purpose of it is *di-
dactic*. What can be done in a primary or secondary school
classroom, Pastor Vega does through the use of a privileged
medium, even more popular than formal education. But
although that is a noble and entirely valid reason, it's not
enough to make a film a work of art. We have, then, that

---

138 Anthropologists do not agree with this discovery, of course. The masculinity of the Sun and the femininity of the Moon (of the Earth) are not
solely due to Romance languages but belong to ancient cultures from
many parts of the world. It would suffice to recall Vedic representations
(it is very difficult to confuse the *linga* with the vagina of Ma[dre]-Ganga
or the Ganges), Mesopotamian, sub-Saharan African, and, of course,
those of ancient Egypt (obelisks and pyramids are phallic and divine elements that emulate the rays of the sun fertilizing the earth, just as in
Mesoamerica, etc. All of these, I understand, predate the *Romance languages*.

139 Barret had noted that "we can explore the historical construction of
the categories of masculinity and femininity without being obligated to
deny that, historically specific as they are, they nevertheless exist today
in systematic and even predictable terms." To which de Laurentis responds: "However, Barret's conceptual framework does not permit an
understanding of the ideology of gender in specifically feminist theoretical terms" (8), as if it were obligatory and necessary to do so in those specific theoretical terms she has chosen to understand reality.

neither the theme nor the inferred "purpose" have anything to do with art; but art needs a theme and a purpose. When both are clichés, they at least serve as an excuse for the creation of the artistic work. *Portrait of Teresa* does not lack this other dimension—the artistic—perhaps the central one among all the dimensions of a film.

Now, to the point. Cuban cinema, as in Gutiérrez Alea, by 1979 had already addressed "the situation of the ideological oppression of women in a machista society." Up to then, this concern had gone hand in hand with others of equal importance: "the oppression of the working class" (El mégano), "the consciousness-raising140 of the individual through history" (Lucía), "the consciousness-raising of the individual of the social transcendence of their revolutionary ethics" (Manuela), etc. Even Memories of Underdevelopment seems to be a turning point in Gutiérrez Alea's production. If The Death of a Bureaucrat was ironic, it was still a positivist critique of an "old order" that survived in revolutionary Cuba. But an order to be destroyed. In *Memories of Underdevelopment*, the direction Cuban society—the Revolution, the Utopia—will take is no longer so clear; moreover: its ending is skeptical and even pessimistic. The artist, like the protagonist, has lost faith in the future of utopia and has also lost faith in man (the new

---

140 "Conscientization" understood in the sense given by Paulo Freire.

one). He sees more continuities than changes, especially within Cuban society itself.

It could be said that in all these films, the issue of gender is always present and that *we cannot remove it without altering the final result of each production*. However, this concern did not overshadow other specific considerations about history, revolution, utopian society, and present society. Politics, up until *Memories of Underdevelopment*, though without fully falling into propaganda or radical criticism, was an explicit theme.

We will see that in *Strawberry and Chocolate*, all these elements will be revisited by Gutiérrez Alea141. Even in his last film, *Guantanamera*. But in between, something has happened. What has happened in *Portrait of Teresa* with Alea's other concerns?

So, what is this significant—ideological—omission? In *Portrait of Teresa*, we see a Cuban society that is "happy," singing and dancing in the streets. A free and creative society, giving space to the working class to create art and to have fun. A fully participatory working-class society in assemblies, with a tolerant body that listens to everyone equally—including women, represented by Teresa—and moderators who are an example, not only of democracy

---

141 I understand that *Strawberry and Chocolate* is another excellent opportunity to discuss the problem of gender, as this "liberated" perspective is here freed from its sexual component, that is, male-female as "logical" synonyms of masculine-feminine.

and tolerance for others' opinions, but of genuine concern for others' problems. The militaristic tone of their voices, which stand out from other "voices" when they are not in command positions, seems to indicate to us confidence and security in their efficiency and ideological clarity in favor of freedom and participatory democracy, rather than a probable state of political oppression. All of this does not mean we should take it «a priori» as overacting or an unreal state. We will assume that these scenes are entirely representative—as representative as those of *PM*.

But something is missing. In this perfect world—humble but (or precisely because of that) perfect—the only discordant note is Teresa's Name. Teresa's coworkers—men and women—beyond being "within" a gender ideology, are portrayed as lucid and aware of Teresa's problem (just as in *Manuela*, the representatives of the State embody moral consciousness; in this case, as in the other, it is an "evolved feminist consciousness"). In this sense, the *simplification* contrasts with the *problematization* of *Memories of Underdevelopment*. If any explicit political, ideological reference appears, it is not to pose a question or to express the complexity of a social plot, but simply to "illustrate," like a travel company putting a photo of a palm tree on a poster to promote a Caribbean island. Resources such as the intercalation of political news on the radio or television are reduced to that: to *resources*, the repetition of a technique that in earlier films, like those of Gutiérrez Alea, were part of the central *problem*. The imitation of a melodramatic

193

television character by a man (giving a flower to a woman to win her back) does not consist so much in a reflection on the role of cinema itself, on the "modeling" of the individual through culture, on the interpellation of gender, but in a critique of the male individual who is unable to understand his situation in the domestic and sociohistorical spheres. For Cubans, direct references to the government are simply a subliminal reminder that the State and the Revolution participate in the critique of the "machista" who is lost in an ideal state of social harmony, outdated by the history that changes and evolves. Teresa's drama is presented with a single, universal cause: the machismo of her husband. With this cause removed, there would be no conflict in *Portrait of Teresa*, which reminds us that something is missing.

In this way, in my view, a significant *silence* is imposed regarding other types of oppressions that are synthesized in each of the particular oppressions—of gender, class, race, thought, etc. The reality is—strategically, we can conjecture, without inferring any intentionality on the author's part—simplified in favor of the status quo. By reducing a social drama to something for which I am not the cause, I confirm it. This "silence" exists and is significant because it is neither accidental nor necessary: *Portrait of Teresa* could have maintained its focus on the social problem without omitting the other dimensions of the social conflict, *even if these dimensions were independent and did not affect the gender dimension.* After all, if we removed the rumba dances

194

in the happy streets of Havana or took out a dozen other elements that complete the framework or context of the filmic text, it wouldn't affect the central issue—the gender issue—. And yet, there was time and space for all of that.

If we refer to Althusser's concept of interpellation, here the central interpellated is the viewer: the Cuban social order of the time is feminist. Not because it is part of the revolution, as it is imposed in *Manuela*, but because the reformulation of genders is preexisting and, in a way, independent of the revolution: it will happen with or without it. But the Revolution must take possession of it by representing it as its own.

Teresa de Lauretis takes up this idea of Althusser, but the actors here are others, almost opposite:

This is, of course, the process described by Althusser with the word *interpellation*, the process whereby a social representation is accepted and absorbed by an individual as her (or his) own representation, and so becomes, for that individual, real, even though it is in fact imaginary (12).

The same idea will be taken up by Zaverzaeh, applied specifically to Western capitalist culture. In *Portrait of Teresa*, we could directly understand that "a social representation" refers to the construction of Teresa as a (subjugated) woman by a machista tradition, represented by her husband, "and absorbed by an individual as her [...] own representation." Nevertheless, we can see that this "social representation" is also the "representation of the Revolution as the engine of female liberation" while the individuals absorbing this ideology are not the actors in the film but its viewers. Consistent with this interpretation, we can cite de Lauretis herself when she quotes Foucault: the repression of sex by state (or societal) institutions, far from repressing sexuality itself, produces it. Using a similar paradox, we can say that the critique of *Portrait of Teresa* does not critique a social order but rather legitimizes it: a Revolution in its conservative stage that resorts to "reforms," not within its own core but within the object of its own discourse: Cuban society.

LEJANÍAS

Jesús Díaz, 1985

Cuban cinema not only has the appeal of its "imperfection"[142], as a theoretical formulation and practical realization, but also the rare allure of austerity and, above all, the appeal of its alternative originality: even when it doesn't reach its finest moments, its saving grace is its particularity as a non-commercial proposal, as a humanizing will of art as reflection.

In several of the recent films we've watched, the dialectic of interior-exterior spaces persists, where the former represents the family conflict and the latter the symbolic context of Cuban identity: a Havana always seen from the perspective of balconies and rooftops—*Lucía, Memories of Underdevelopment, Portrait of Teresa*—. The city is the symbolic object, the subject of reflection, of its characters. It is the living space that seems to share the destiny and anxieties of its inhabitants, so far from the geometric and abstract images of the panoramic shots of North American cinema about their cities. In commercial films from Hollywood (generally North American), when someone goes

---

142 Represented, according to Chanan, by the "green" third of the ICAIC (p. 430), since it is very difficult to speak of an "independent Cuban cinema"; at least not with the necessary resources to form an important tradition.

up to a rooftop, it's to escape someone or chase them. The North American rooftop is the marginal space of urban consciousness where conflicts are typically resolved with a weapon in hand or the hero prevents someone from jumping into the *void*. If it's not a luxurious Penthouse, they are not livable spaces. And, what's worse, no one even wants to live there, not even the marginalized. The marginal spaces in this American aesthetic are always the sewers, never the heights. *Lucía II* could well have used this device, as its plot unfolded during a moment of armed conflict, where its protagonists were active agents in the conflict. But no. Aldo goes up to the rooftop with Lucía in a moment of poetic climax where the "action" is interior, not exterior. In these scenes, the rooftops are not a marginal space with respect to the law, nor are they an excuse for action that entertains a sedentary viewer, but rather the "open and elevated space" that functions as a multiple vantage point. In none of these cases has the *ascent* to the rooftops been an empty action, but rather it has given its physical space to the symbolic space of the narrative and its protagonists. In all cases, it is an existentialist attitude of *observation*, self-observation, and thus of *reflection* as "social individuals."

Regarding the dominant space in Lejanías—the interior space—Chanan points out that "Díaz uses the spatial texture of the apartment to reveal the distances that separates his characters on various different levels" (420).[143] The mother's apartment—now the son's—is the temporal and spatial confluence point of the entire drama and all its intertextualities. On the old television, a woman sings the bolero "Veinte años atrás" (*"today I represent the past and I cannot accept it"*), followed by the tango of Carlos Gardel, "Volver"—returning from exile to Buenos Aires, "with a withered forehead"—who at some point should have said "that twenty years are nothing." This intertextuality is redundant, but it accentuates one of the themes that provokes the familial—and ideological—conflict: the return.

The mother, who seeks to recover her son's love—whether as an end or as a means to repair her own conflicts and feelings of guilt—says, perhaps too explicitly: "I will fill you with *things.*" To which the son of the Revolution protests: "Mom, I don't need anything." At another moment, the frivolous and consumerist attitude of the mother, asking about products available in the market, is met with a similar response from her son: "Here we have problems, but no one is left without work, school, or medical care."[144] She asks her daughter-in-law "what is it that

---

[143] Which, if it weren't for the fact that we have already seen several Cuban films (and because it is not spoken in English), this space might predispose us more to expect a proposal similar to Alfred Hitchcock.
[144] When Reinaldo and his cousin go up to the rooftop—a place for reflection on the city and, therefore, on society—what most catches her

you most desire in life", to which Ana hesitates to respond[145]. Enough time for Susana to confirm, once again, her ideological type: "*to have* what one did not have: a house, perfumes, expensive clothes, to travel..."[146] The verb *to have* is key, which is why Ana will take it up again to invert its meaning and, consequently, perform an ethical inversion: "*to have* Rey", she responds[147]. This same idea is confirmed as a new *ad hoc* (in the sense that it does not imply a necessary continuity in the dialogue) when Susana asks Aleida why she kept coming back to her son, despite his alcoholism.[148] The response: because she loved

---

attention in the urban skyline is a modern building that turns out to be a hospital, a symbol of Castro's Cuba: advanced and democratic medicine.

[145] I have heard the same question in "street" surveys on Miami TV. The answers are almost invariable: a car, clothes, a house, etc. But this is not just a characteristic of Cubans in Miami. I have heard exactly the same thing from young Americans who, in luxurious churches, intended to evangelize Latinos who did not know English.

[146] Aleida's daughter's question about the number of gifts and why they will be returned is a pretext to enunciate a higher ethical law: "we don't need them to live." Of course, this universal principle is also being used by the discourse of the Revolution.

[147] Surely the names "Reinaldo" and his nickname "Rey" are symbolic: Reinaldo is a Cuban, and all are kings in the sense that they possess the dignity that was once monopolized by the nobility (much to Ortega y Gasset's dismay). We could also find a connection with Aldo (Lucía) and Aleida with Alea, considering the great intertextuality of Cuban cinema itself present in this film, but perhaps this would be an overinterpretation if we do not find more evidence of these symbolic connections. As Chanan has already noted, there is a great intertextuality in reference to other films by Alea (422).

[148] Alcohol is an omnipresent element in all the psychological conflicts of the male protagonists in these films.

Rey. "He's so beautiful. For you and for me, he's the most beautiful." (Which recalls the popular saying: "For a mother, there are no ugly children") The connection is obvious, and Susana understands it without delay. She defends herself by saying that she did not abandon her son. However, her excuses are weak or, worse, unjustifiable: "I had no choice." The father's voice on the recorder provides no better reasons for the abandonment; they only appeal to the sentimentality of someone who is dying and asks for his son's forgiveness. "*I did not abandon you* —says the father—; *what happened was...life.*" It was obvious that, since it was a recording, the protagonist would rewind to let the audience hear such a phrase that reveals a lack of reasons and a lack of scruples and feelings of solidarity. His voice is equally overacted and seems implausible, but it is more than likely that this was a deliberate result, that is, significant. Aleida takes the voice of the Cubans to respond to her mother-in-law: "what you did, no one understands, ma'am."

At times, the acting is melodramatic, especially in the case of cousin Ana, reciting a poem by Lourdes Casal about New York and exile with a rhythm of classic overacting. However, this is another opportunity for a new discursive and problematizing proposal. I understand that it is no coincidence that New York is compared to Miami, with a clear disadvantage for the latter. Ana is appalled by the city of exiles. New York is the symbol of the United States, but it is also the most diverse and least conservative face of this country. Miami not only represents the anti-Castro exile; for the rest of Cubans and for much of the world, it is the symbol of the Susanas: lumpens and compradors —to use adjectives from the classic rhetoric of militant Marxism— who sold their dignity, their family, and their homeland for money. They are the audience of Don Francisco, measuring happiness and success by the dollars they receive on the Wheel of Fortune. The idea of dignity is, above all, the greatest asset that Aleida and Reinaldo possess. Her rejection of the gifts is done with an absolute phrase: "here [in Cuba, in the Revolution] there is dignity." Ana also declares it: "Miami, where your mother lives, I can't stand it." In Miami, there is no poetry, no art, nothing that isn't a Cuban appetite for material wealth. In contrast, Ana is presented as a young woman with feelings. If Reinaldo was forced to stay, she was forced to leave. They are both victims of their parents' ambition and, therefore, she can endure the American but not the Cuban-Americanized.149 When Reinaldo bids farewell to

---

149 I am unaware if there are studies on this, but perhaps we could say that Miami is the city most beloved by Cuban exiles and the most hated by the rest of Latino immigrants—not to mention Latinos from Latin America.

his mother and cousin, he will show more affection for the latter, confirming the earlier idea.

But Susana is not only the embodiment of selfishness and materialism. Her "wealth" is her poverty. Susana confuses the trivial with the important, clothes and "things" with feelings. Susana is the prostitute mother, the ideological whore, the past: her codes and her scale of values are those of the old Cuban upper class, selfish and superficial. This is represented in her ethical parameters: "Why did you marry a divorcee", "I would have preferred if she were a maiden", etc.[150] The same codes of the corrupt past represented by Uncle Jacinto, the Cuban who did not go into exile but betrays the moral ideals of the new Cuba, of the new man.

This story can be considered "exceptional" within the political and social context of the time. However, last Saturday, October 1st —do coincidences exist?— I saw on American Spanish-language television, *Univisión*, a report on the immigration of Guatemalans to the United States and the broken families left behind in their home country. One of the boys who had stayed in Guatemala had been abandoned by a mother who had gone to seek better fortune in the north. The boy's words —resentful, indifferent to his mother's late annual returns— aligned exactly with

---

[150] This same past is evident when she comments on how well the priests regarded her Aleida's intelligence, showing that she had entrusted her son's education to the Catholic Church.

the plot of *Lejanías*. The mother's justifications were as convincing as Susana's and her dying husband's. But in this case, of course, the Cuban regime was not mentioned as the cause of the problem. In this case, the explanations were all "personal", the result of an "immigration phenomenon." And nothing more.

Havana

Jana Bokova, 1990.

Introduction

With documentary pretensions, *Havana* is a historical *narration* and a political discourse on (post)revolutionary Cuba. Paradoxically, this narration tells us that the Revolution has been a counter-revolutionary, anti-reformist, conservative, and immobilizing process. According to it, what has changed with the Revolution are the men and, above all, the discourse. A "Cuban spirit" remains in the living traditions of the lower-class Blacks and in the dead traditions of the former upper-class Whites.

The discourses, the narratives of reality —political and literary— are the center of this film and the center of its implicit thesis: reality depends on a narrative, which can be constructed through images but, above all, is a narrative of words. The most explicit form of constructing an artistic discourse that carries an implicit thesis and an explicit story is done through the mosaic method. No resource is discarded to tell the same story. However, the narration of *Havana* is a counter-narration to the Main Voice of the "text" (fiction) called *Cuba*: Fidel Castro.

Havana does not tell us that *history is always a questionable narrative*, but that the narration of the Main Voice of the text *Cuba* is unreliable: the viewer possesses (thanks to Bokova) the necessary perspective to appreciate the contradictions of the Main Narrator and the "narrated facts" (the images captured by the camera). In other words, the viewer must trust the new narration, the contestatory narration of Havana.

In *Havana*, the narration is both constructor and protagonist of the artistic phenomenon: it is constructed with two basic elements: words and images, political discourses and urban images, literary texts and paintings. [151]

In this sense, it is no coincidence that we have three important groups of verbal narrators: (1) Cuban writers, (2) unnamed Cubans, and (3) Fidel Castro, the voice, the main narrator, the omnipresent narrator of the mother of all fictions: Cuba.

The voice of Reinaldo Arenas denouncing "Closed, closed, everything is closed," while he walks through the city and later finds his typewriter and the world opens up, is a philosophical, existential declaration about the writer and his art. This aligns with the film's ideology: reality is a narrative construction. The word is the main protagonist: protagonist in constructing the film and protagonist in constructing and destroying the Revolution. Arenas recalls

---

[151] Perhaps it is no coincidence that Jana Bokova's latest film is based on the story of another writer, a paradigm of Latin American fiction, "Diary of a Story" by Julio Cortázar.

the last words of Lezama Lima: "In words lies salvation" [The parole Ends]

But we know, by this same dynamic, that words are both salvation and damnation, denunciation and evasion. *Havana* reflects a "special period" but does not make it explicit. Throughout the filmic narration, the historical and economic factor disappears beneath the discourses. Everything is alluded to, and even hidden. The reading (hermeneutic, like any deep reading) must resort to a metatextual study to understand that none of the narrations —represented by the three groups— is reliable.

The beginning of *Havana* is deliberately a cliché of Cuban cinema: images of the triumphant revolutionaries. As if that weren't enough, the film *Before Night Falls* will use these same historical images with the same narrator — Reinaldo Arenas— conditioning them according to his marginal perspective. It's no coincidence: Havana will seek from the outset a contestatory narration to that of the Castro regime, crafting it from the margins of Cuban society.

The contrast will be the response to the desire for "continuity solution" in the ideological narration.[152] The contrast will be one of its main resources. As a cinematic technique, it's another cliché; as a resource, it will be no

---

[152] Frederic Jameson: "[...] the deepest, most contradictory, but also the most urgent level of Lyotard's book: that of a narrative which —like all narrative— must generate the illusion of 'any imaginary resolution of real contradictions' (Levi-Strauss) (xix).

less effective than any originality. While the well-known historical images at the beginning of the revolution show political and social events, significant for Cuba as a problem, the voice of the narrator contrasts with its subjectivity, sometimes incredulous, nihilistic, at other times detached from the events: "I start whistling... I run along the royal road, I call you out loud." Unlike a political verse by Pablo Neruda, here we have a poetic concern of a pseudo-romantic, neo-baroque nature. Only moments later will the narrator, the poet, return to refer to the political event with an "indifferent rejection": "flags, papers, rags, flags, flags..." The images of the triumphant revolution (collectivity, society) contrast with the introverted narrator, provocatively subjectivist, uninterested, almost indifferent. The social, political discourse contrasts with the interior monologue of the narrator. The credulity of the people with the nihilism of the poet.[153]

The narrative contrast suggests an absence, a disconnection between discourse and action, between the vigor of the political discourse and the idle passivity of people killing their time on the Malecón, between the main narration and the images, between the voice of the Great narrator and the voice of the writers. Havana also rescues the images of a Havana that could coincide with the political agitation of

---

[153] This image portrayed by *Havana* does not correspond to reality, if we consider that Reinaldo Arenas joined the Castro Revolution in 1958 and collaborated with it as an official at the José Martí National Library.

the revolutionary triumph: the immobile Havana, almost indifferent, surrealistically empty, ghostly.

To complete its purpose of contrasting plastic narrations and discursive narrations, the film will —literally— direct its camera from the historical center to a "conventillo" in ruins but still inhabited. In this movement, there is also a chronological shift of twenty-five years. In this way, the narration, through the voices of its protagonists, places us at the heart of the historical time of the Revolution, of its own work.

The technique used is another cliché: someone behind the camera asks the questions, and an improvised inhabitant of the tenement answers. The questions are typical of a surveyor: "What is your profession?" "Do you have relatives in the United States?" "Do you live here? Where?"

Answers: "I've lived here since 1975. I came here for work, ten years ago."

Enough. That's what we wanted to know.

The plot of this chapter?: the collapse of the tenement. The theme?: passivity, hopelessness, contradictions. The *contrast.*

"We're on *stand by*," says one of the characters. "If the house collapses, it collapses."

And then? What happens if it does?

"The government will take care of it."

The narration of the characters is led by the interviewer again and again to the theme of the *collapse*, of *passivity*, of *waiting*: waiting for the government to fix the housing; waiting for the government to fall, etc. Waiting.

Then the inevitable question, as demagogic as the Voice it seeks to denounce: "Would you like to keep living here?"

And the contradictory responses, loaded with prefabricated discourses:

1: "Of course not, I'm here for who knows what reason."

2: "[Here I am] happy, happy, happy."

We humans are contradictory in our diversity; our expectations differ, sometimes radically, even within the same family. This makes the intersubjective contradictions unsurprising. However, in the narrations of the interviewees, we can never overlook *the conditions that generate the discourse*, depending on whether one is for or against the regime. Cuba is a narrative construction with a strong political tone, both internally and externally. The narrative fracture is separated by an unfathomable abyss with no historical resolution. Therefore, none of its contradictions is as dramatic as the discursive contradictions, its narrative antinomies.

After the interviewer insists on her need to know if those poor Cubans had relatives abroad, a voice overlaps the images to denounce the lie of the Great Voice's narration: "all that about fallen in battle is a lie. They died in the barracks. They invented the combat story." Once again, the narration overlaps with someone leaning against a door or a column.

The tenement is Cuba in Havana, and the interviewees are the characters, shaped and deformed by the Revolution.154 According to the rest of the film's narration, passivity will be presented as (1) the ambiguous result of a Cuban characteristic, one of its cultural traits, while also (2) the consequence of twenty-five years of Revolution, of the regime's state paternalism.

—The neighbors are very good. She was sleeping, and the room collapsed on her.

Not only the house (Cuba) is in ruins, collapsing. The language is also one of its reflections, this metaphor of Cuban society in decay: its articulation is difficult, ruinous in its grammar —if not also in its intonation. It is no coincidence that most of the interviewees are elderly; mostly over eighty years old. The eighty-year-old Spaniard who was in Cuba for 68 years is grateful for everything Cuba has given him.

But since this is a Neo baroque film, the contrast and the contestation will be repeated resources. Another of these contrasts is the socio-racial one. If the tenement is the ruined city of the Black people, the mansions still maintain the *glamour* of the '50s. They were and continue to be enclaves of white people. White people as unproductive as, apparently, the Black people in the tenements shown by

---

154 The tenement house encapsulates much of Cuba's history. It is its metaphor, its witness; it was the residence of a count, then a convent, the building of the official gazette, and later state property.

Havana, who are unable to react to the collapse of their own houses. Upper-class whites and lower-class Blacks: both are presented as unproductive and passive in the face of their own reality. In *Havana*, there are no proletarians. ([155])

Apart from the socio-racial contrast, we can observe others, through the technique of *superimposition*, in the same narration: The dancers dressed in yellow ([156]) seem like surreal characters amidst the shantytowns. They come and go, contrasting with the ruins and with the discourse of the Great Narrator, only to finally be justified when the carnival parade takes place. The carnival, besides being a strongly baroque element (as baroque as the decay of the tenement), is a denial of other discourses coexisting without political conflict.

Interspersed, we are presented with the interview of the 82-year-old woman. Despite having said she had lived there, in that humble house, for 42 years, the interviewer asks: *"Did you live here before the revolution?"* which shows that it is not information that is sought but rather for the character to complete her portrait: things haven't changed.

---

[155] The (interviewed) characters who speak English represent a fallen upper bourgeoisie. «When I moved to this home...» One of the characters mentions that the house was once exclusive to white people. "It changed a lot, the white people left." Its inhabitants were employees of the Eastern Company. The old woman hums a Christmas song typical of the United States.

[156] It is likely that the yellow color was a choice by Bokova or simply a defect in the video, as its quality was not the best.

Reality hasn't changed. Yet, the discourse is different. The narration is different: the elderly woman changes her tone. Despite her age, her voice takes on the enthusiasm and energy of the Great Voice:

"Life is ten times better. Now we all eat the same, equally. I live content with the revolution. —in an affected voice—: My family were all revolutionaries... We had the confidence that we were going to win. God in heaven and Fidel on earth. Homeland or death. *And tell everyone what we are enjoying.*"

The narration of happiness, indifferent to any adverse reality, is discursive. It is no different from the narration of exiles who demand a *"success-story"* narration in the United States. As is the case with Guillermón in *Balseros*.

The discursive contrast appears with the son. In an almost inaudible voice, he asks: "Why are you saying that?" His silent face also reveals suppressed discontent. The gestures of the elderly woman reflect old arguments with the young man: "It's the truth," she says, "Am I lying?"

1989: the Great Voice expresses itself in all its symbolic strength: as if it were being reproduced and amplified by urban speakers, it overlaps any image. The camera cannot escape it. The inhabitants cannot either. But the camera is not innocent. While its ears accept the Narration of the Revolution, its eyes deliberately fixate on the contradictions. They choose, select, contrast. While The Voice speaks of "the socialist development, roads, rings, one, two, three, four, five, six..." the baroque nature of the film composition does its work: indifferent dancers, the poverty of the houses, of regressive underdevelopment. "I would like to know— says the main Narrator— if in the United States, if in Europe, in the Netherlands, there is an organization of this magnitude." And later, a significant slip: "This people, this country, will know how to be consequence... consistent with their history."157

Part of the narration is constructing reality through omissions: how it is elsewhere is unknown. For a foreigner—and for the film's viewers—it is a joke; for the 82-year-old woman, it is a reality.

Another contrast: while the Voice of the island praises the "political consciousness" of its people, willing to "die before retreating," two dancers parade in their carnival costumes. These images represent a contrast, on one hand, and on the other, they are the classic embodiment of the idea of irrationality, of simulation, of spectacle, and of parody.

The carnival is baroque par excellence. At the moment we see this parade of the people, we hear the baroque narration of Lezama Lima: the excessive use of adjectives, the ornamentation. If the baroque has been contestatory since its origins, the poet's narration is also so: "a house without anyone" (They cross[ed] the line).

---

157 Consequence implies passivity, like the effect of an external cause (history); consequential, on the other hand, implies a persevering, free consciousness. According to psychoanalysis, we should not trust the correctness of the discourse but rather the spontaneous statement.

Part of that same baroque quality is integrating even the most opposing fragments, in a desire for "atonality." The presence of Afro-Cuban songs and dances is itself a fragment that opposes the poems of the old upper bourgeoisie. But they also declare by themselves the ideology (or reading of reality) of the baroque, of the Afro-Cubanism of Nicolás Guillén:

"*I am Yoruba [...] I am Mandinga*"[158]

Slave tradition:

Some commanding

Others commanded

[but in times of celebration, of rituals, of carnival:]

all mixed together

[mestizaje (mulataje) and syncretism]

San Benito, Santa María...[159]

But *Havana* is not just the contestatory discourse against the Main Voice. It also presents a tradition in a far

---

[158] In the Southern Cone, "Mandinga" means "devil," and I understand it as a Christian gaucho interpretation of the African pantheon. Similar is the term «Shetani» in East Africa, which biblical tradition understands as "demon" but among the Swahili is simply part of one of their gods in the polytheistic pantheon. Today these *shetanis* can be seen represented in carvings of «pau preto» in Mozambique, for example.

[159] We have been together from far away,/ young, old,/ black and white, all mixed; / one commanding and another commanded,/ all mixed; /San Berenito and another commanded,/ all mixed;/ black and white from far away,

all mixed; /Santa María and one commanded, /all mixed; /all mixed, Santa María, /San Berenito, all mixed, /all mixed, San Berenito, /San Berenito, Santa María,/ Santa María, San Berenito /all mixed!

215

from innocent way. The Cuban tradition—according to the film's discourse—is hedonistic. One of the interviewees boasts of his improvidence: "I spend everything I have"

While the song confirms: "I enjoy myself / and I don't care what they say"

Or the aversion to work, the philosophy of the cicada: "I don't want a machete / because I'm anti-machete." It is sung by another elder, another 87-year-old Black man.

Havana spends a disproportionate amount of time on the singers: the mosaic captures a large piece representing the past (the times of Machado) and the Afro-Cuban (musical) tradition. Then another large piece of similar characteristics: the bodily dialogue of Black dance, characteristic not only of Havana but also of some corners of the Atlantic South America.

"What are your plans?" the journalist asks.

"None. *I live in the present*" the girl responds, insistently, as if she were aware of her own life philosophy. This aligns with a tradition but contradicts the Revolution.

Visual art, symbolism: Columns are inevitable. In the urban center of Havana, these architectural elements predominate, part of a neo-baroque and colonial architecture, with Doric pillars and semicircular arches. Yet the columns are the main protagonists. Alone or accumulated in a central perspective, where the Cubans lean their slender figures. Beyond their phallic connotation—as the Hindu *lingam* might explicitly suggest—here remains the plastic force of power. The father, the Great Voice is omnipresent.

So is the vertical solidity. It is not the slenderness of the Gothic but the *horror vacui* of the Baroque. Despite the poverty, the adjective fills everything. Cubans cannot speak without leaning on this solidity.

Alejo Carpentier's narration ("Journey to the Seed") is an allusion not only to the magical character of Cuba, to the dreamlike, but also to the idea of chronological "regression" alluded to in the city.

Dispensable observations

The poet Pablo Hernández Fernández—a symbol of the old upper class. His poetry is a verbal game and part of the divorce between the individual and society:
"The complicated world simplified my life."
Simple people complicated my world."
Then, other traits belonging to the past bourgeoisie:
"I love the paintings. I have a collection of coffee cups."
Mercedes Linz (Dulce María) "I wrote verses when young; when old, it no longer fits." This formula is typical of the 'afrancesados' for whom the poetic paradigm is not Neruda but Arthur Rumbad. This is confirmed by her 19th-century definition (like the house, like her reality) of art: "Fans are the most beautiful and useless things. Beautiful things are often useless."[160] And her ideological definition:

---

[160] Paradoxically, industrialist art (the *Arts and Crafts,* of William Morris) emerged to respond to this ideology, and a fan was precisely one of the

"There was always a passion for freedom in my house," as if there were someone in the mid-20th century who wouldn't say the same. The pretentiousness and anachronism of this "lady" are evident in her own language: "It's better not to talk about Havana. *Forgive me.*"

Úrsula Maceara Benítez: "I knew wealth in all its stages"

Another: "I'm Catholic; my son is communist"

Intertextuality insists on superimposing Caribbean history (the literature) with images of the present: "the landowner left the group [and] calmly shot those who protested" And then, the key to the reading: "history may be true or false, but the times made it believable"

Perhaps the character who demonstrates the greatest social and historical consciousness is the painter son of Ponce de León, which does not align with this idea of "apprentice" or "illegal practice of the profession" suggested by the system. But since the Official Narrative is monolithic yet does not disdain any argument, they imprisoned him for leading "an unusual life." Responding to the Great Voice's narrative, for which all problems originate outside, the painter says "we must fight for our own problems, here inside." In contrast, the hallucinated discourse of the "mambí" against the U.S. invasion.

"useful" elements where this new art of the late 19th century was expressed

Another painter: imprisoned in 1973, "I don't know why." Despite there being no charges against him, they left him in prison for "six months, so he could think"

Voice-over. "For more than twenty years a Duke of Alba..." in bed. "Technocracy and distrust." We no longer suffer anything. They allow us to take pills and calm down"

Multiple marginality of Arenas (Cuba-United States): "From a legal standpoint, I do not exist. I am a dissident, not religious, I am homosexual and anti-Castrist."

Havana is a mosaic, but its narrative fractures when it spends so much time on Reinaldo Arenas: that is material for another documentary, as indeed happens years later.

Recurring song (*Lejanías*):

"Hoy represento el pasado, no me puedo conformar"
("Today I represent the past / I cannot settle")

Writers mentioned
Lezama Lima
Virgilio Piñeda
Alejo Carpentier
Nicolás Guillén
Reinaldo Arenas
Cabrera Infante.

BALSEROS

Carles Bosch and Josep Maria Domènech, 200

When the context is Cuba the text is under a political lens that demands a definition of the same genre. This implicit demand is the product of a deformation produced by the Manichean history of the last fifty years. Consequently, cinematic productions have responded to this political simplification by taking a position according to the only available sides: on this side or the other. When we watch a Cuban film, we generally cannot abstract ourselves from this demand. From the beginning, we question the position of its producer: From what ideological viewpoint is the film being narrated? We know that this viewpoint will be (1) in favor of the communist regime, (2) against the communist regime, or (3) relative, in favor and against both. This, which seems like a tautology, is not: in any case, the political factor remains omnipresent and demands a judgment.

I understand that *Balseros* has a rare merit: how to make a film about Cuba, about the social and political issues of Cuba without taking sides? But more than that: how to make a film about Cuba's political problem without the political element becoming the underlying theme? Balseros seems to have achieved this by placing human drama at the center, in such a way that it prevents us from defining the political stance of its creators. If, at the beginning, anti-

Castro viewers applauded the images of communist misery that justified the rafters' adventure and the apparent "American Dream" realized in the second half of the film, all of that quickly comes into question, and an ineffable ghost crosses many of the stories: their efforts have taken them from communist misery to consumerist misery. The drama of human complexity begins to displace the political drama. The exiles are not depicted so much as people forced to leave the country by force, but rather as people who abandon it to pursue material dreams that they sometimes achieve (modestly) and other times do not. After several years of hardship in the United States, the "American Dream" is not destroyed, as it was never a simple hope but a myth. And myths are not destroyed by personal reality. However, the paradox of the new system becomes clear: to give the family in Cuba everything they want (or need), one must first forget about them. As one of the counselor characters says, to help others, you first have to be in a good place yourself. But that "good place" never arrives, and the struggle for survival becomes a forgetting of the originally stated purpose.161 On the other hand, freedom has a price;

---

161 A Cuban veteran advises and instructs the newcomer in the art of capitalist survival: "you have to solve your problems and you don't have time to worry about others. And since you always have problems..." "Working, working, day and night," what could be the lyrics of a song is the slogan promoted for the serving classes, those who can only aspire to "exemplary worker of the week," with their small photo of honors stuck on a fast-food wall. Or what is the same: "the company prospers, we prosper, and everyone is happy." Applause.

it almost always goes through the clergy of capitalism: the lawyers, who are inaccessible to the rafters and to the poorly paid service workers.

The lack of freedom of expression is mentioned as a problem, but at no point is it dramatized as poverty is.[162] On the contrary, the public festivities of raft-building seem to indicate a folklore promoted by some tourism ministry. Which is partly logical. The film is aimed at a consumerist audience for whom "freedom of expression" is not central; what is central is "purchasing power." None of the rafters is an intellectual, one of those writers hiding on the island, a rebellious idealist, or an artist who has been liberated by some circumstance. The rafters of Balseros are not refugees of conscience but capitalist refugees: all of them want "to progress," to have "a house, a car, and a woman" or "to give the girl whatever she asks for." The phrase painted on a boat "In God We Trust" represents the promise of material prosperity in the United States; not God, because in Cuban slang, He is called by any other name. Also, the lyrics of the rumba that accompanies it: "may it be as God wills" does not refer to God but to luck, to (American) fortune that

---

[162] It is significant that the same film, surrounded by political connotations, is exhibited and awarded by both God and the Devil: *Balseros participated in the 24th International Festival of New Latin American Cinema, Havana, in 2002, being awarded as the best "foreign documentary." Also in Miami, the following year, it participates in the International Film Festival and receives the Audience Award*

these person-characters will try to achieve in Miami, in the Bronx, New York, in Grand Isle, Nebraska, and in Albuquerque, New Mexico. Kaminski quotes Coper: "If it's about ambition, we were all born in the wrong country."

Balseros belongs to the documentary genre; it is testimonial and it is "reality show." In other words, it is the synthesis of a tradition and a novelty of 1990s television. The voice-over narrating the story that is displayed in images is a constant in other Cuban films. Sometimes that voice is personal; other times, it is a form of voice of conscience, an interior monologue. As in previous films, the intertextuality of other media (especially television) contextualizes the text and complements its narrative. In Memories of Underdevelopment, Fidel Castro and Kennedy appeared; in Balseros, Fidel Castro and Bill Clinton appear. In all the others, Fidel Castro appears. Another element that emphasizes the testimonial style is the selection of five people who narrate their adventure on the rafts (Rafael Cano, Oscar del Valle, Mérycis, Míriam...) in such a way that at the beginning, it makes us doubt whether they are professional actors or common people reenacting their own lives. Another is the interviews, such as those who are denied visas by the United States,,163 which has a real and direct reading: the rafters are the product of an administrative policy on both

---

163 One of the interviewees says, at the door of the North American embassy and after being denied the possibility of entering this country legally: "The only option I have left is to take to the sea."

sides. All of this is supported by the insistence on specific dates, with day and time marked on the screen as the facts of an investigation into that collective fiction we all call reality are marked. All of which is confirmed by the use of familiar faces on Hispanic television in the United States, of "real" programs, and of lawyers who really are lawyers.

To conclude, a theoretical observation: Kaminski presents an idea that Amarill Chanady had already analyzed in *Latin American Identity and Constructions of Difference*:

Because of the "impossible unity of the nations as a symbolic force," any construction of a coherent view of the nation, or sustained strategy of nation-building, necessarily leads to homogenization. As Renan writes, "unity is always affected by means of brutality." What that means is not only that the non-hegemonic sectors of society are "obligated to forget," and concomitantly obligated to adopt dominant cultural paradigms in several spheres, but that "forgetting" is the result of marginalization and silencing, if not annihilation (xix).

However, I do not find the argument that the notion of the nation is defined by exile or diaspora to be solid. The use of examples from Benedetti, Peri Rossi, etc., is valuable for describing one form of definition of nationality, belonging, "nationalist" subjectivity, etc. But they are not sufficient for a more general conceptualization of the central terms it attempts to define (homeland, motherland, identity, history, national myths, etc.). I could argue that the definition of nation (like the definition of identity and of person) is closely related to the definition and exclusion of the "other." Anyone can intuit that without ever having read J. Derrida. In this sense, yes, exile plays a fundamental role—but not a decisive one.

1. Introduction

The question about the gendered nature of *Balseros* leads us to the question about the narrative nature of Cuban reality. Is *Balseros* a documentary or fiction? In one way or another, Cubans know they are the protagonists of a (dramatic) international spectacle that rarely focuses on the issue of Human Rights—as we will see later—manipulated from both banks for their own propaganda purposes. Advertising is a fragmented narrative, repetitive, with few ideas, with the will, like the myth, to simplify a reality and adapt it to a simple and convenient response.

For Jean-Françoise Lyotard, "the narrative's reference may seem to belong to the past, but in reality, it is always contemporaneous with the act of recitation." (22) Undoubtedly, this observation is linked to the need for legitimation—and self-legitimation—of every narrative, whether it is macro-political or the personal and domestic representations of the "chess pawns," as one of the characters of *Balseros*, Guillermo, puts it.[164]

---

[164] The reference to chess is taken up by Carlos Bosch, in an interview given to the BBC on February 24, 2004: "Back then, in '94, Fidel Castro

If we answer that *Balseros* is a documentary because it deals with events that really happened, we are mistaken: "the representative" is never the reality, but the idea of "sample" held by its creator. If we think that Balseros is a documentary because the protagonists do not "act" but "live" their own lives, we are also doubly mistaken: First, because the mere presence of a camera inevitably introduces a distorting element into the subjectivities of those who "act their own lives"; Second, because the protagonists are characters, beings as real as they are fictional, who act out an idea, a story, a narrative. If "reality" does not fit that narration, too bad for it. "I have said that narrative knowledge does not give priority to the questions of its own legitimation and that it certifies itself on the pragmatics of its own transmission without having recourse to argumentation and proof."165 (Lyotard, 27)

This essay aims to approach the film *Balseros* (Cuba-Spain 2002) from the theoretical perspective of Jean-Françoise Lyotard. If I had to summarize the reading of this film in a brief quote from this French thinker, I would probably choose the following: "Even more modern was

---

challenged the United States to take in 30,000. That chess game between (former U.S. president) Bill Clinton and Castro is the backdrop to the balseros crisis." Perhaps we should question this subaltern idea of "backdrop."

165 "Narratives are fables, myths, legends, fit only for women and children" (27)

his suggestion [that of Aristotle] that scientific knowledge, including its pretension to express the being of referent, is composed only of fragments and proofs—in other words, of dialectics." (29) The precision we will make here will be to change the term «modern» (since it is written in lower-case and does not refer to Modernity) to «Postmodern», in its reference to late capitalism.

Another effort we will make, though only as a sketch, is to identify the same *narrative* strategy in both antagonistic discourses. In the words of Mas'ud Zavarzaeh, "ideology critique violate the principle of uniqueness" (3); for its detractors, this type of reading (materialist, structuralist, Marxist) is "reductionist." However, "the actual reason for these attacks [...] is that ideology critique displaces the individual by pointing out the global structures that in fact construct his seemingly 'natural' uniqueness and freedom." (4)

Another idea of Zavarzaeh that relates to Lyotard—though ideologically opposed—is his conception of tale: "in producing the tale, the spectator learns the ideological syntax of his culture (its class relations) and demonstrates his ability to provide coherent tales—as maps for dealing with the real—and thus proves he is a symbolically competent and ideologically reliable person." (11)166

---

166 "The tale in the film is not in the text itself (is not a positive entity): it is not determined. Therefore, is not accessible through an analysis of formal properties." (18)

A synthesis of both thoughts, initially incompatible, can be achieved by considering *Balseros* as belonging to an intermediate genre between fiction and documentary and, at the same time, by considering its actors as spectators (Lyotard) and its spectators as actors (Zavarzaeh). This idea is suggested, though not explicitly formulated, in the film Memories of Underdevelopment (Cuba, 1968). That is, by definitively destroying the boundaries between the work (the film) and reality (its referent), we finally understand the dialectical relationship between the reader and the writer and between both and the ideological struggle between a dominant culture and a resistant (or subaltern) one.167 In this way we will have a narrator-reader, both in the spectators (readers) and in the protagonists (character-writers).

Zavarzaeh formulated it this way: "Films (and other works of art) are related to reality, but this relation is not one of reflection, reporting, or even interpretation. Rather,

---

167 In another space, we should distinguish between "dominant ideology" and "hegemonic culture" (Gramsci). On the other hand, Zavarzaeh himself seems to leave open that door which produces an "ideological struggle": "One way to allow other tales to surface is to use the device of renarrating to displace the overt tale." (25) The emphasis is ours. Renarration (or rewriting) is a political weapon and not simply a hermeneutic exercise. "Renarrating as a reading strategy, then, is a political act that calls attention on the construction of the real and furthermore opens up a space for contesting the existing." (91)

films are related to reality because their actually participate in the cultural act of producing the real." (95)

Of course, this expository ambition is much more ambitious than the materialized result in this brief and urgent work. But we can see it as a sketch, an approach for future problematization.

2. The Characters

Tens of thousands of Cubans took to the sea in 1994. Thirty thousand of them were housed in Panama by U.S. forces. Another twenty-eight thousand in Guantánamo. Mericys González, Oscar del Valle, Rafael Cano, Miriam Hernández, Guillermo Armas, the protagonists of *Balseros*, are some of those tens of thousands scattered later across Miami, the Bronx (New York) Grand Isle (Nebraska), and Albuquerque (New Mexico). In the homonymous book, Balseros (1997), Felicia Guerra and Tamara Álvarez-Detrell had used the same technique, though transferred to paper: a limited set of witnesses, rafters from 1994 in Albuquerque, New Mexico, and Miami, Florida. The result of this "document" is a very different story from the one proposed by the 2002 film.168

---

168 The book *Balseros*, despite (or perhaps because of) having been written by two PhDs from the United States, not only lacks art but also lacks any rigor. The excuse of "protecting the identity" of the interviewees leads to omitting their last names. Since we cannot even see their faces or hear the tone of their voices, we can only consider it as "testimony" or

Joseph María Doménech, along with other Catalan journalists, personally covered (part of) the events of 1994, which left him with a significant volume of recordings that would later be used in *Balseros*. It is important to note that from this selection of stories, difficult to consider representative solely due to the disproportion in numbers, the filmmakers decided to exclude another story from the film: it was about a ninety-year-old blind man with a twenty-year-old wife.169 The reason given by Doménech was the extreme particularity of this case. In other words, Doménech sought believability so that it would be understood as a representative truth of a much more complex reality.

However, the artistic proposal is valid and inevitable: one cannot narrate the stories of a thousand or ten thousand people in two hours aiming for greater "representativeness." This reminds us that we are facing an artistic work; not a statistical reality, more akin to *National Geographic* or *Discovery Channel*. That is, *Balseros* proposes the rescue of a sensitive aspect of an unfathomable reality, even by the numbers. This does not make it any less or more real, but rather it carries the same reality, exposed from another point of view, from an artistic—and human—perspective,

---

"document," as they are presented, through a great act of faith—republican faith. The publication of such a work can only be explained by an appealing ideological market.

169 Diary *Ámbito Financiero*, Buenos Aires, September 9, 2004.

with all the questioning that a proposal of this type necessarily entails.

3. The narration of the film

At the beginning, *Balseros* revisits one of the unavoidable components of the tradition of Cuban revolutionary cinema: the "voiceover" narration, a blend of political reflection and existential questioning: «Summer of 1994... following the fall of the USSR, Cuba's economy suffers. Shortages.» Following this is another recurring element of the same tradition: archival footage, taken from some television archive: the theft of «La Lancha de Regla», followed by the violent protest of the people over the detention of the boat. «From there, many things happened», says the narrator, suggesting that this was the catalyst for the phenomenon of the 1994 rafters. These two elements, the monologue of the absent narrator and the archival footage, can be seen in almost the same sequence in films like Lucía (1962), Death of a Bureaucrat (1966), Memories of Underdevelopment (1968), Lejanías (1985), Havana (1990), Before Night Falls (2000). Some of these, like Before Night Falls, were not produced in Cuba, or Balseros' director and screenwriter were not Cuban; nevertheless, it seems that the subject matter recalled the characteristics of revolutionary Cuban cinema.

One of the things that happened was the confirmation of another post-revolutionary Cuban tradition: critical cycles, the expulsion or opening of borders to emigration (1965, 1980, 1994) accompanied by the same manifestations against the "traitors" and the repeated «let them go». Another was the re-evaluation of U.S. policies of "open doors" for Cuban refugees[170].

But the narration of *Balseros* is not composed solely of images. Although less explicitly than Havana (Bokova, 1990), here the contrast or the sequence of images will do the same narrative work. A kind of "contrastive narration"—if I may—can be appreciated in the moment when Rafael's family is engaged in the worship of Santería, which is then followed by the image of a letter on Oscar's lap as he travels in a plane. Clearly, one can read: "Church World Service." Then, the same camera completes its own narrative: beside it, almost allegorical, a straw hat (guajiro) wrapped in an American flag, which almost recalls *Azúcar amarga*.

This type of resource is frequent and forms part of the narration of *Balseros*, that narration which falls under the domain of Doménech's pen and outside the control of the narrative voices of the protagonists.

---

[170] As we will see later, the Clinton administration (or the "government" of Clinton, to avoid the old democratic euphemism) officially ended the "Open Doors" policy. However, this end has been very relative: Cuban refugees continue to have privileges compared to refugees from other countries.

4. the characters' narratives

The characters' narratives, though conditioned by the scissors of the producers, form a central part of the film's narration. That is, the film, by selecting the characters' voices, is constructing its own narration. Even so, we can still distinguish between one type of narration and the other. Especially when we assume that these voices, although selected, have not been *produced* in a classical sense, by a screenwriter. That is, we can still read between the lines; a hermeneutic reading *independent* of the filmmakers' intentions is still valid. A hermeneutic reading, of course, with an ideological goal (as we cited Zavarzaeh). Perhaps this aspect best represents the "documentary value" of the artistic proposal, as it is the element, the text least manipulable, at least consciously.

An example we can consider is the legend painted on one of the rafts: In God We Trust. While the allusion could not be more direct—to the United States, to the Dollar as a symbol, as God—its semantics reveal this absolute ideological dependency: the order is not natural in Spanish; it is in English—In God We Trust. As if that were not enough, one of the protagonists repeats it, in case there were any illiterate spectators: "Remember that in God we trust." In this way, a material, economic objective is "divinized" with a supposedly transcendent, spiritual narration. From the modern narration of Marxism, from the socialist discourse of fraternity and sacrifice—proto-Christian and a kind of

234

atheistic Christianity—we easily move to the discourse of
the individual, of hedonism and economic success (represented by the dollar, symbol of a materialistic religiosity;
few things are as absurd and contradictory as identifying
the Christian God with money). Consumerism is, or can
be, a reflection of hedonism and individualism, but from a
Marxist reading, it would only be the expression of an economic need for market expansion. In *Balseros*, there is a
scene that dramatizes this moment. While Misclaida and
Juan Carlos argue about which car is better, one of *Balseros'*
voices suggests to Juan Carlos that he kiss it (her), which
Juan Carlos misinterprets by kissing the car. Jean-Françoise
Lyotard understands it in the following way, as a response,
though debatable:

This breaking up of the great Narratives [...] leads to
what some authors analyze in terms of the dissolution of
the social bond and the disintegration of social aggregates
into a mass of individual atoms thrown into the absurdity
of Brownian motion. Nothing of the kind is happening:
this point of view, it seems to me, is haunted by the paradi-
saic representation of a lost "organic" society. (15)

The idea that Lyotard seems to refute is confirmed by
the advice of the Cuban uncle living in New York to Oscar
(perhaps the most applauded line of the film): "In the capitalist system where you have to solve your own problems
first before solving someone else's problems. As problems
come every day, one cannot be concerned with the problems of others." *Balseros* will show us, later, an Oscar lost in

the delinquency of New York, forgotten by his family in Cuba.

In Guillermo's case, we can see a dramatic change in his discourse. We can understand this change as a "self-narration" that seeks to justify him before others and before himself. While the first images we have of him show us a rebellious and indiscriminately critical man, by the end we will have another version of him, which we could call a "domesticated version," if it weren't for the great deal of judgment and value embedded in this definition.

When we see Guillermo at the U.S. Interests Section, a voice narrates what we are already seeing: "full of people, hour after hour."

Someone complains:

"That's what I don't understand; that there are so many obstacles, both on one side and the other."

"What do the Americans say? What is the truth? Or are we just pawns in a chess game."

"This is the fourth time I've come here," says Guillermo, now with a gray beard. "If they don't resolve it today, I have no other option but to throw myself into the sea. I have a raft on the roof of my house."

And later, finally resolved to "jump":

"This vessel is named... after my daughter. Nizeli María."

In contrast to the first Guillermo, we are introduced to Rafael Cano, aspiring from the start for the life of a perfect petit bourgeois. His declaration of intent is confirmed, ironically, by a song that follows him everywhere: «*buy my-self a house, a car, a good woman...*» Like Guillermo, but in the opposite direction, Rafael will eventually drift into religious fanaticism that contradicts his original dreams. (And even his initial religion).

Rafael, this person-character, both inside and outside the film, is narrated by his own sister, which reveals a psychology confirmed by her own words: "And because he's noble, he got off [the raft]." The initial failure does not interrupt his dreams or the refrain of the song: «*a car, a house, and a good woman...*»

In opposition to this materialist pretension, the discourse of the regime arises. While not unreasonable, the fact that it is Fidel Castro who argues against this superficial materialism weakens the criticism itself:

One of the most serious problems and the most negative legacies left to us by the developed capitalist world are its consumption standards. [A car advertisement] has made the beggar, on the streets of a capital in an underdeveloped country, dream of the car, the blonde or the brunette, and they associate it, moreover: if you don't have the car, you don't have the woman. (Conde, 155)[171]

---

[171] Later, Fidel Castro himself makes another observation not without logic (especially if we consider it was made in 1988): "What would happen if every Chinese family had a car, and if every Indian family had a car, and if the 400 million inhabitants of Latin America had a car?" (Conde, 157) This interview conducted by the Galician writer Alfredo Conde suffers from excessive complacency toward his interviewee. At no point

The *voice* of *Balseros* —seemingly neutral, like that of a professional interviewer— asks Misclaida's sister, off-camera: "Do you mind if we film you while you're out there looking for men?" to which she responds that she doesn't mind. This reminds us of another foreign documentary, Havana, by Jana Bokova, another European for whom learning about the life of a prostitute and simultaneously portraying her as a human being is a morbid discovery, which surely isn't the case for Cubans.

Misclaida is many characters, different depending on the story being told. In *Balseros* as in Havana, we have only one version. But just as we can understand a main narrator in a fictional work, we can also understand these characters in their fatality. The first Guillermo's mention that Cubans, the rafters, were pawns in a chess game is a metaphor that extends throughout much of the film's narration. Especially when the "problem" is resolved with a bilateral agreement between the governments of Fidel Castro and Bill Clinton. This macro-political reality is only briefly reflected in news clips that are easily recognized by the audience, both Anglo and Hispanic in the United States.172 It's about

does Conde cross the line of a good interviewer; at no point does he risk an inquisitive question.

172 Even the young immigration lawyer is a recognized professional, a habitué of television programs like *Don Francisco* and *Cristina*. In this sense, Chanan understands that "the mass media and new communication technologies produce new forms of addressing the public, in the form of vertical flow, wherein social dialogue is embodied in reductive genres and

the movements of the main pieces, the queen, the rooks, and the bishops. The game will end, as always so far, in a draw. However, in the process of measuring strengths, several pawns will fall. Balseros constructs the narration of this game from the perspective of the pawns, which allows us to identify as the audience and, perhaps for that very reason, makes it more difficult for us to have a more critical reading of the strategic moves of the game. Only one tradition persists in the narration of the characters, one we've seen repeated since the 16th century in Ibero-America: in the end, authority acts in its own interest; the cannon fodder are, ultimately, always the same. The system of powers never operates for the benefit of Human Rights but for political and Economic Interests. Everything else is discourse —ideological narration. Misclaida fails in her first attempt to take to the raft; she returns due to bad weather but then must stay in Cuba because "we were caught by the law that said you could no longer leave." Days earlier, her mother had represented high politics by urging her daughter to make a decision, because those in power "go to the bathroom to pee and immediately reach an agreement." Which

---

stereotypes (and open to manipulation by political forces who have learned how to play the game). Fascism, capitalism, and communism inherit this situation and deal with it differently. Capitalism develops practices such as public relations and new management intended to mold and bend public opinion by less than honest means, while, as Walter Benjamin put it in the closing words of his best-known essay, fascism renders politics aesthetics, and communism responds by politicizing art." (Chanan, 16)

is a way of desacralizing and discrediting the power that decides their fates.

Eight months later, Miriam speaks to her mother from Miami through a recording. It is significant that her first words do not focus on emotional, family, or domestic matters, but rather on an immediate political self-justification: "I'm a little nervous. I left because, you know, life there wasn't easy..." We assume her mother already knew this, but Miriam feels the need to confirm it by repeating the narrative of the process that led her to leave her mother alone on the island. This narration, we can assume, considers not only her mother as the audience but also the potential viewers of Catalan TV. "I wanted to give my daughter everything I couldn't have, I wanted to give my daughter everything she deserves; whatever she might ask for one day, I wanted to be able to give it to her," Miriam insists, perhaps unaware of the strong materialistic undertone of her justificatory discourse.

However, the contradictions of the capitalist system soon emerge. Just like the advice Oscar received in New York, Miriam experiences the paradox of her destiny firsthand: she thought she would come to the United States to reclaim her daughter, but she couldn't because she didn't have money for a lawyer.173 The critic Guillermo who left

---

173 This paradox, "Working, working, day and night," was noted and formulated by Ernesto Sábato in 1951: "The theorists of mechanization argued that machines, by freeing man from manual labor, would leave

Cuba needs his own narrative to justify himself. The excess of work allows him to do nothing but work and distract himself (to regain energy and continue working). Everything, as Althusser would say, driven by the reproduction of the means of production: "the company thrives, we thrive, and everyone is happy."174

5. The politics implied

While we can say there were times when arbitrariness didn't need justification if it possessed force or the

---

more free time for spiritual activities. In practice, things turned out the opposite, and each day we have less time." (55)

174 "[...] To exist, every social formation must, at the same time as it produces, and precisely in order to produce, reproduce the conditions of its production." (106)

The reproduction of labor power takes place outside the enterprise. Its qualification must occur apart from production: "Unlike what happened in slave and serf-based social formations, the reproduction of the qualification of labor power tends (it is a tendential law) to be ensured, no longer 'on the go' (learning within production itself) but increasingly apart from production: through the capitalist school system and by means of other procedures and institutions." (110) "[...] the reproduction of labor power requires not only a reproduction of its qualification but also, and simultaneously, a reproduction of submission to the rules of the established order, that is, a reproduction of submission to the dominant ideology by the workers and a reproduction of the ability to handle the dominant ideology appropriately by the agents of exploitation and repression, so that they also ensure, 'through words,' the dominance of the ruling class." (111)

monopoly on violence, it's hard to assert that the need for legitimacy is unique to recent centuries. For Althusser, both elements still coexist. Though somewhat redundant, he sums it up this way: "the (repressive) State apparatus «functions through violence», while the ideological State apparatuses function through ideology" (124).

Lyotard sees in contemporary imperialism the existence of an immanent trait: "It is the entire history of cultural imperialism from the dawn of Western civilization. It is important to recognize its special tenor, which sets it apart from all other forms of imperialism: it is governed by the demand for legitimation." (27)

For our part, we do not see a moment in our time where "legitimation" is not an essential requirement. It probably wasn't considered in the times of Genghis Khan, but in the rest of history it has been almost uninterrupted. It is today for any ideological group, just as it was previously the basis for the religious and social dominance of the church. In our time, this legitimation, as Lyotard suggests, is based on discourse, on the construction of a narrative that overcomes its own contradictions, "an imaginary resolution of real contradictions." (xix) However, nor can we say that it is the private property of power, of a dictatorship, or of imperialism.

When in *Azúcar amarga*, one of the characters, Bobby, injects himself with AIDS-infected blood, he does so in front of a camera, holding the government responsible for the act. The move resembles another more real one: when

Reinaldo Arenas commits suicide in the United States, he leaves a letter directly blaming Fidel Castro for his death. He does not blame the tragedy of his illness (he also suffered from AIDS), nor the marginalizations he endured in Miami—as he acknowledges in Havana (1990) and in *Antes que anochezc*a (1994).175 This gives an idea of how reality can be viewed through a purely ideological lens. This is demonstrated, both on one side and the other of the ideological divide, in the interviews conducted by Jana Bokova in Havana: experience is irrelevant; what matters is the narrative each person constructs to justify their life, their sufferings, or their happiness. This does not mean that everything is relative, but that when we speak of Cuba, we cannot for a single moment suspend the pre-established political-ideological discourses.

Havana shows the same economic decline as *Azúcar amarga*. Superimposed and contrasted with these images, there are also the speeches and painted slogans on the walls announcing a triumph that never came. In the case of the first, there is also an intention of documentary, as in *Balseros*, but also a series of interviews that aim to accentuate these contrasts between the individual (absorbed) discourse and the surrounding reality. The reality has not changed. However, the discourse is different. The narrative is another: an elderly woman is shown in poverty while she

---

175 "From a legal standpoint, I don't exist. I'm a dissident, I'm not religious, I'm homosexual, and I'm anti-Castro."

delivers an existentialist speech. Despite her age, her voice takes on the enthusiasm and energy of the Great Voice: "Life is ten times better. Now we all eat the same, equally. I live happily with the revolution. —with an affected voice—: My family were all revolutionaries... We had the confidence that we would win. God in heaven and Fidel on earth. Homeland or death. And tell everyone what we are enjoying."

The narrative of happiness, indifferent to any adverse reality, is discursive. It is no different from the narrative of exiles who demand a *success-focused* narrative in the United States. As is the case with Guillermo in *Balseros*.

The discursive contrast appears with her son. In an almost inaudible voice, he asks: "Why is she saying that?" His silent face also reveals repressed discontent. The elderly woman's gestures reflect old arguments with the young man: "It's the truth —she says— Am I lying?"

A similar contrast, a similar narrative of political success, independent of experience, can be seen in *Balseros*, when in an urban speech, the officialdom repeats over loudspeakers the worn-out words of «Homeland or death, we will triumph. Long live Raúl, Long live Fidel. Long live Cuba libre». The first two phrases are just advertising: it is a declaration of war. The last phrase, of course, is a fundamental part of the ideological narrative, which serves both Greeks and Trojans alike.

We cannot overlook at any moment the political and politicizing component of the narratives that in some way refer to Cuba. Even less so in cinema, a mass medium compared to written text. "Politics in Cuban cinema," says Chanan, "is not a subtext that either filmmaker or the critic can include or leave out; it is the inevitable and ever-present intertext of the aesthetic, and its constant dialogue with the political." (12) Later, he confirms this with another idea: "[It is] impossible to understand Cuban cinema on a theoretical basis that separates politics and art [...] This dialogue allows that cinema screen to become more than either propaganda or a diversionary space, but a crucial preserve of public speech [...]" (18)

Although *Balseros* cannot be classified entirely as part of 'Cuban cinema', we can understand that it does not escape this reality, this implicit 'political reading' of the text called Cuba.

6. Metatextual data of the conflict

From the beginning, we have sided with the thesis of the political-ideological component in the structuring of the narratives that intersect in *Balseros*. The same can be said about those narratives that are implicit in the filmic text but do not appear represented, at least not denotatively.

The macro-political level does not escape these Machiavellian rules of the game. According to the authors of the study "The End of the Cuban Contradiction in U.S. Refugee Policy,"

> Between 1959 and 1995, U.S. refugee policy towards Cubans was not based on humanitarian equality, as eventually mandated by the Refugee Act of 1980, but was defined by an anti-communist political agenda. [From 1962 until 1994] over 1 million Cubans received preference over refugees from other nations through an 'open door' to the United States" (Nackerud 177)

As the authors further state, Cubans were not the only refugees migrating to Florida. In 1980, 60,000 Haitians had entered Florida seeking refuge. During the same period, half a million Central Americans arrived in the United States seeking political asylum. While Cubans received almost automatic refuge, "people asking for sanctuary from right-wing dictatorship supported by the U.S. government had to prove a well-funded, individual fear of political persecution." (181) And further: "As demonstrated by the Mariel Crisis, the preferential treatment of Cubans continued despite the Refugee Act of 1980, which was intended to bring U.S. refugee policy in line with internationally developed humanitarian norms." (182) The same observations are made by Walt Vanderbush and Patrik Haney in "Policy toward Cuba in the Clinton Administration," for whom U.S. policy regarding "refugees" in their "humanitarian" struggle has had "a double standard relative to Cuban exiles" compared to other refugees, such as Haitians (392), and by Kevin McHugh, Inés M. Miyares, and Emily H. Skop. (505)

However, starting in 1994, due to the events recounted in *Balseros*, there was a shift that marked the official closure of the previous "open door" policy. The 1995 agreement consisted of granting 20,000 U.S. visas to Cubans. Part of the agreement included Castro's commitment.176 to refrain from encouraging this mass emigration, meaning he would keep the borders closed. (181)

According to the authors of "The End..." from the University of Georgia, the 1994 balseros crisis was a joint consequence of the effects of the U.S. embargo and its "open doors" policy, exclusively for those Cubans who dared to reach the U.S. by raft. (186) The contradiction is expressed by Guillermo himself when, outside the gates of the U.S. Embassy in Cuba, he laments that both countries have placed the inhabitants between a rock and a hard place. Guillermo will forget all these circumstances once he settles in the U.S. and adopts a success-driven discourse that justifies him, representing him as part of the exiled group. In this way, we can see that narratives are transmitted like language: regardless of the diversity of immigrants with different languages; sooner or later they end up speaking the same, the hegemonic one.

Access to data is, and will continue to be, the prerogative of experts of all stripes. The ruling class is and will

---

176 One can find the "Joint Communiqué on U.S.-Cuba Immigration Agreement" from September 4, 1994, in U.S.-Cuban Relations in the 21st Century, by Bernard W. Aronson and William D. Rogers.

continue to be the class of decision makers. Even now it is no longer composed of the traditional political class, but of a composite layer of corporate leaders, high-level administrators, and the heads of the major professional, labor, political, and religious organizations. (Aronson, 14)

In line with this, Frederic Jameson writes that "for Habermas, indeed, postmodernism involves the explicit repudiation of the modernist tradition —the return of the middle-class philistine or Spiessburger rejection of modernist forms and values —and as such the expression of a new social conservatism." (xvii) Part of this drama, this Manichean manipulation of the powers in dispute, lies in the simplification of alternatives. For Carlos Bosch, director of Balseros,

the exodus of the Cuban rafters must be interpreted as an economic exodus, [but] as unfortunately they are only allowed to return in dribs and drabs, they automatically become political emigrants, in the sense that they did not want to go into exile but left, like most migrants in a moment of despair, anywhere. And the closest place was the United States. (Favella)

On the other hand, the initial quote from the book *Balseros*, by Felicia Guerra and Tamara Álvarez-Detrell reveals, for reasons that escape its authors, the background of the Cuban drama: "The Cuban condition becomes a relatively simple dilemma: either one stands in solidarity with the palace of the Revolution in Havana, or one lives in Miami."

(12)177 This quote is representative of the entire book. Although this book implicitly confirms this dilemma, it cannot resolve nor is it aware of the arbitrariness of its premise. And here we can understand not only an ideological radicalization, not only a simplification, but the dogmatic profile of the interviewees: their opposition to a regime they consider unjust is resolved with Cuban-American propaganda, which we could define as the simplest narrative, often lacking in history or discourse. The artificial option of being "on one side or the other" resolves in an authoritarian and arbitrary manner that there can be no other options. Why do Cuban refugees not choose another country? Even within the United States the majority choose Miami. Why? For reasons of survival, one could say. Yet, why, to oppose the Castro regime, from a standpoint of human rather than political or economic vindication, must one cross the line and stand on the side of the United States, of Miami's closed ideology?

One of the interviewees in Guerra and Álvarez-Detrell's book, Eduardo, summarizes this attitude: "[After Hermanos al Rescate picked me up] they asked me if I wanted to go to Puerto Rico, to my family's house. I said no, that for the moment I didn't want to go. And they sent me to Albuquerque, and here I am." (Guerra, 21)

---

177 Quote attributed to Fogel and Rosenthal: *End of the Century in Havana*.

In all the interviews, the oppression of the Castro regime is discussed. Which is valid. But that doesn't mean it isn't also a justification with other motivations. Why don't any of these testimonies include an anti-Castro figure who also rejects American ideology?

There is a significant narrative difference between the film *Balseros*, by Doménech, and the book Balseros, by Guerra and Álvarez-Detrell. The former is told from a critical ideological perspective toward Miami's ideology; the latter, though more explicit, is a completely opposed narrative. The only thing they have in common is the claim to be "documents"—documentaries—based on interviews with Cubans who survived the 1994 exodus. In any case, the protagonists are instruments of two conflicting machines.

Bibliography

Althusser, Louis. *Writings*. Barcelona: Editorial Laia, 1974.

Aronson, Brenard W. and Wiliam D. Rogers *U.S.-Cuban Relations in the 21st Century*. New York: Council of Foreign Relations, 1999.

Azúcar Amarga. Dir. León Ichaso. Dominican Republic-United States, 2004.

Balseros. Dir. Carles Bosch and Josep Mª Doménech. Perf. Mericys González, Oscar del Valle, Rafael Cano, Miriam Hernández and Guillermon Armas. TV Catalana. Cuba-Spain, 2002.

Chanan, Michael. *Cuban Cinema*. Minneapolis: University of Minnesota Press, 2003.

Conde, Alfredo. *A Conversation in Havana*. Madrid: Ediciones El País/Aguilar, 1989.

Guerra, Felicia, Tamara Álvarez-Detrell. *Balseros*: Oral History of the Cuban Exodus of '94. Miami, FL: Ediciones Universal, 1997.

Havana. Dir, Jana Bokova, Cuba-United States, 1990.

Lejanía. Dir. Jesús Díaz. Cuba, 1985.

Lyotard, Jean-Françoise. The Postmodern Condition: A Report on Knowledge. Minnesota: University of Minnesota Press, 1984.

McHugh, Kevin, Inés M. Miyares and emily H. Skop. "The Magnetism of Miami: Segmented Paths in Cuban Migration" *Geographical Review* 87 (1997): 504-519

Memorias del subdesarrollo. Dir. G. Gutiérrez Alea, ICAIC, Cuba, 1968.

Nackerud, Larry, Alison Springer, Christopher Larrison and Alicia Isaac. "The End of the Cuban Contradiction in U.S. Refugee Policy" *IMR* 33-1 (1999): 176-192.

Sábato, Ernesto. *Men and Gears. Reflections on Money, Reason, and the Collapse of Our Time*. Buenos Aires, Emecé, 1951.

Vanderbush, Walt and Patrik Haney. "Policy toward Cuba in the Clinton Administration." Political Science Quarterly 114 (1999): 387-408.

Zavarzaeh, Mas'ud. Seeing Films Politically. New York: State University of New York. Press. 1991.

HISTORIAS MÍNIMAS

Carlos Sorin, 2002

Sometimes, the title of a work, whether literary, cinematic, or of any other artistic genre, alludes to a reality opposite to the one intended to be expressed or depicted. This is the case with the film "The City of Fable" or several surrealist paintings, where the title aimed to negate the evidence of the image. On other occasions—most of the time—the opposite occurs, and the title serves as an introduction to the work itself.

This is the case of *Historias mínimas*. In this film, a handful of deliberately simple and provocatively humble stories are brought together, supported by an austere and "neorealist" technical approach. Perhaps what these three or four stories have in common is not the syllogistic logic of detective or mystery genre plots, but something more akin to everyday reality, dominated by contingency rather than the "necessity" of events. They share a common space (a nearly unknown town in the middle of the Argentine Pampas) and, probably, a national characteristic that has progressively taken root in the societies of the Southern Cone: a certain air of resignation and failure persists in this film from the beginning and is confirmed, in a chilling way, at the end.

In *Historias mínimas*, there is a deliberate attempt to emphasize solitude. Its protagonists live in a town-island of the Pampas (a sea-form without water). Modernity passes violently by their side (every so often, the silence and humility of the place are interrupted by the roar of a bus or a truck that pass without stopping for a moment: they pass and are seen by its inhabitants, with composure). But modernity passes and also *splashes*: the town has satellite dishes and television. While the old man with the dog amuses the children by moving his ears, a humble young girl begins to dream of the lights of a television program, to which she is invited by chance.

Argentina of the "it can't be done" is reflected in the old man's son's refusal when he expresses his intention to go look for his dog. But the old man, in an attitude of a stubborn elderly man and rebellious teenager, embarks on a quixotic journey. It is quixotic not only because of the difficulty of the task (his dog is three hundred kilometers away) but also because of the apparent absurdity of his goal. However, what seems absurd to everyone is not absurd to the old man: "That dog is the only one who knows who I am," the old man confesses almost at the end.

I believe this journey also serves Soria to introduce the old man's character into a contrast with the modern world (the beginning of the journey with the young biologist) and also with two psychological types very common in Argentina and Uruguay rural areas: the idleness of public officials (the guards) and the unconditional friendship of the rest of the characters.

Another of the narrative threads that articulate one of the three minimal stories is the journey of the birthday cake. The character who aims to win over a woman is obsessively meticulous, which he himself recognizes. This mania for perfection and the details that can affect a long-awaited event leads him to a resounding failure (he himself destroys the cake that cost him so much effort and that caused so much trouble for others, and he destroys it also due to a misunderstanding). In this minimal story, Soria resorts to some repetitions. To underline the obsessive nature of the character, he repeats the same situations several times: each time the birthday cake takes him to a place, and while he speaks to a woman, the camera and the character stop at the photographs of the husbands hanging on the walls. "I lost my wife because of jealousy," the character admits while watching a similar scene on television. The solidarity of the characters, and especially of the secondary characters, is repeated.

Perhaps it is in this minimal story and in the character of the salesman where the idea of being lost in a labyrinth becomes most evident: in a dialectical labyrinth, in a psychological labyrinth, in a physical labyrinth (the salesman has traveled more than two million kilometers) and, perhaps, in a social and political labyrinth—even though politics and social issues are never explicitly addressed.

The ending confirms the suspicion: the main characters do not triumph, as in Hollywood; or if they do, their achievements are minimal, achievements that resemble failure more than success: the old man has reached his absurd goal, the salesman returns after having vomited the cake, after having frustrated his objective on his own, though unintentionally, and the young girl returns from her long journey to fame with a ridiculously insignificant prize.

In recent discussions with critic friends, who enthusiastically support the emergence of new technical resources in art as a way to expand expression (the quasi-redundancy is worth noting), I have maintained that artistic expression does not necessarily depend on new and sophisticated technical resources. I believe one of the basic premises of art has been the search for economy in means of expression. The greatest works of art demonstrate this: *less is more*. In this way, it becomes clear why black and white photography can be (and often is) superior to color photography: black and white emphasizes form, and it is here that the renunciation of one resource becomes a deepening of expression. This was the case, I suppose, with the film "Schindler's List" and others where the feat was not in adding special effects but, precisely, in subtracting them. What is a Haiku if not literary economy brought to its maximum expression?

Although this film is not excessively driven by musical resources, music appears as a subtle and repetitive element with which the viewer ends up associating the stories. The use of close-ups is repeated: the expression of the faces is important (even when the dog is the protagonist), especially the face of the old man who speaks little and expresses much, the complete opposite of the salesman and the young girl. The movement of the camera often supports the idea of an aggressive wind, at times accentuating the notion of exposure and vulnerability.

The renunciation of sound, sometimes of dialogue, to uncover what an excess of sounds and words usually covers, is one of its constants. *Historias mínimas* is neither the first nor the last film to make use of this resource; but it is a beautiful example of wise continuity. We know that since the end of the Middle Ages, continuities have not been well received in art, that it is novelty and patricide that have become the objects of cult and veneration. However, when continuities belong to that small set of minor masterpieces, the battered and underestimated human spirit is grateful.

www.ingramcontent.com/pod-product-compliance
Lightning Source LLC
Chambersburg PA
CBHW072341090426
42741CB00012B/2875